CW00725619

Eminent Hungarians explores, in a mainly lighthearted way, fifty famous historical and contemporary personalities associated with Hungary. In celebration of Hungary's accession to the European Union it connects their life stories to reflections on the present.

eminent hungarians

by Ray Keenoy

To Sarah Joanna Dorothy,
Ray Keenoy, Oxford,
all the best 2005

BOULEVARD

Eminent Hungarians
©Boulevard Books 2003
First published 2003 by Boulevard Books
71 Lytton Road
Oxford OX4 3NY, UK
Tel/Fax 01865 712931
email: raybabel@dircon.co.uk
babelguides.com

The publisher would like to thank the Magyar Magic Festival and the
Hungarian Cultural Centre London for their help with this book.

Special thanks to Jackie Wrout and Kate Lonsdale

ISBN 1-899460-06-3

Boulevard Books are distributed in the **UK & Europe** by Drake
International, Market House, Market Place, Deddington, Oxford
0X15 0SE tel 01869 338240 fax 338310 info@drakeint.co.uk
www.drakeint.co.uk and in the **USA & Canada** by ISBS
5804 NE Hassio St, Portland, Oregon 97213-3644
tel 00 1 503 287 3093 fax 280 8832 info@isbs.com

Cover Art & illustration: Jackie Wrout
Typeset : Studio Europa
Printed and bound by Advanced Book Printing, North Moor,
Oxford

Béla Bartók
Eva Bartok
József László Bíró
Brassaï
George Buday
Robert Capa
André Deutsch
Tibor Fischer
Eugene Fodor
Dennis Gabor
Ernő Goldfinger
Harry Houdini
Attila József
Imre Kertész
Kincsem the Horse
Zoltán Kodály
Arthur Koestler
Joseph Kosma
Lajos Kossuth
György Kurtág
Rudolf Lábán
Imre Lakatos
Estée Lauder
Ferenc (Franz) Liszt
Bela Lugosi
Sándor Márai
Margaret of Scotland
George Mikes
András Pető
Karl Polány
Giorgio Pressburger
Joseph Pulitzer
Ferenc Puskás
Árpád Pusztai

Miklós Radnóti
Géza Róheim
Egon Ronay
Ernő Rubik
Claude-Michel Schoenberg
George Soros
István Szabó
Count István Széchenyi
Albert Szent-Györgyi
Leó Szilárd
George Szirtes
Edward Teller
Tokay
Ignatius Trebitsch-Lincoln
Viktor Vasarely
Stephen Vizinczey

eminent hungarians

Béla Bartók

Nagyszentmiklós, Hungary (now Sinnicolau Mare, Romania) 1881–1945 New York, NY USA

Composer and World Music pioneer

A munka dicséri mesterét (The work praises its master)

Bartók enjoyed the casual, spontaneous nature of folk performance so much that he spent most of his life orchestrating and arrang-
ing it for the cumbersome 120-member symphonic orchestra and the
highly trained virtuoso.

One of the many interesting elements in his career is how he pioneered what is known as 'World Music', collecting folk music not
just from his fellow-Hungarians in Hungary, Slovakia and Romania
but also from Slavs, Arabs and Turks. He was a member of the last
Hungarian generation to live in the multinational Central Europe of
the old Austro-Hungarian Empire, and this led him, after the patriot-
ism that gave birth to his symphonic poem *Kossuth* in 1903, to a feeling that the music of all peoples was a joy to be shared and transmit-
ted from one loving ear to another.

The Béla Bartók story is also a love story: the love of a mother for
her son. Paula Bartók was both mother and father to Béla after the
early death of Béla senior and incessantly played to him while he lay
in bed with lengthy childhood illnesses. It's a story of several wives,
too, including one he loved to play concerts with, and of the American composers who rallied round the neglected and impoverished refugee from pro-Nazi Hungary (Bartók refused to accept the country's
highest honour from the hand of Hitler-friendly dictator Admiral
Horthy) and raised money for him in his final illness. Above all, it's a
story of patient love for the musical genius of others, of whole peoples and traditions, expressed in his passionate efforts collecting and
transposing and captured in a famous photograph of him listening
intently to a recording of a folk performance and transcribing it to the
pentagram.

MORE

The Bartók **beginner** might explore:

the *44 Duos* (1931), violin pieces that capture the humour and simple panache of the folk performer;
or the late *Concerto for Orchestra* (1943) with its strong rhythmic element that lets us hear the peasants dance merrily and drunkenly at the wedding of the village beauty to the blacksmith's strong son;

or the majestic and moody *2nd String Quartet, Op.17* (1915–17)

A short web intro:

www.wwnorton.com/classical/composers/Bartok.htm

A standard biography:

Béla Bartók Kenneth Chalmers (1995)

Eva Bartok

Budapest, Hungary 1929–1998 London, England

Actress and mystical disciple

Aki hisz, boldog. Aki nem, okos (Who believes is happy. Who doesn't, wise)

Not an illegitimate daughter of Béla, now why do I always get stuck with this sort of reader! However scandal did seem to follow her around, or did she follow it? Beauteous Eva Bartok, née Éva Szőke (name change ordered by producer Alexander Korda who realised that people like to 'go with what they know' and the Hungarian name they know is, well…), pioneered the celebrity route of the late 1960s and 1970s. A filmstar with forty films under her belt, including *Blood and Lace*, *The Crimson Pirate* (with Burt Lancaster*)*, *10,000 Bedrooms* (co-starring Dean Martin) and the 1963 shocker *The Whip and the Body*, she had close friendships with eligible fellers of the period: the Marquess of Milford Haven, Frank Sinatra *et* (possibly quite a few) *al*, plus holidays in exotic places (not including Budapest). There followed a sudden and dramatic mystical transformation. She renounced the world of showbusiness for an Eastern religious path known as *Subud*, founded by an Indonesian ex-accountant called Muhammed Subuh. Reportedly, *Subud* involves gyrating with other acolytes in a dazed and ecstatic manner until you are 'opened'. That is the moment in which God (or it may be Allah) enters you.

Maybe the simulated weightlessness in her early British sci-fi movie *Spaceways* (1953) or the nuclear ray wielded at her in *The Gamma People* (1956) prepared Eva for this experience, technically known as the *latifah*. Or was it the swallowing of large cocktails with 'ol' blue eyes'…?

Hearteningly, though, and unlike those 'oh-so-spiritual' 1960s popsters Paul McCardy, John Lemon and Mick Jakoff, Eva Bartok remained true to her spiritual insights right up to the end. At her funeral in August 1998, daughter Deanna rebutted the newspaper obituaries' claims that Eva died 'homeless, penniless and alone'. 'I'm here to translate that for you,' Deanna told us. 'Homeless — because she never really appreciated the domestic trappings in life. Penniless — because she didn't really care about money. Alone — she was not, God was with her. I was with her in spirit, and so were many other people.'

And may the force be with *you*!

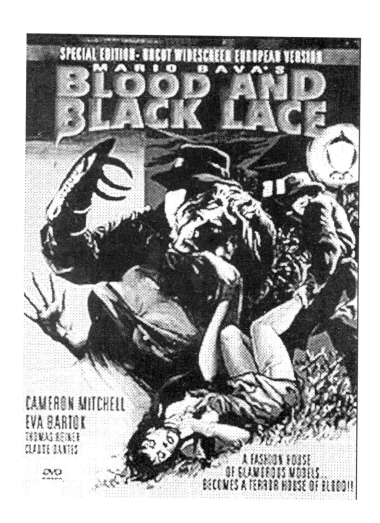

MORE

Many of Eva's **films** are available on DVD or videotape:

www.amazon.com/exec/obidos/tg/detail/-/B00004Z1G1

Eva **wrote** a biography *Worth living for* in 1959, secondhand copies from $5 at www.abebooks.com

A great and true **fan,** M. Omar Martinez of Los Angeles, remembers Eva at: members.tripod.com/evabartok/id17.htm

Official website of **Subud:**

www.subud.org

József László Bíró

Budapest, Hungary 1899–1985 Buenos Aires, Argentina

Inventor of the Biro®

'No man was more foolish when he had not a pen in his hand, or more wise when he had' — Samuel Johnson on Oliver Goldsmith

Yes, it was a Hungarian who invented it (but see below, especially if you're planning to visit Croatia). He did it by making ink sticky and playing with the localized gravity of thin tubes. Surely a lot more useful an invention than the Rubik® cube (except for the terminally uncultured who, before the time of GameBoys®, Walkmen®, mobile phones and other electro-incretinization® devices, had only the cube, or possibly some well-seasoned bubble-gum, to amuse themselves with on the bus, since they were unable to read). Useful, but famously leaky, especially when it's hot in your pocket or when chewed. Best examples of the Biro®: top pocket of office managers; worst examples: bottom of a schoolboy's satchel (don't go there).

A simple, happy story of Hungarian ingenuity and invention — newspaperman László, under pressure from copy deadlines, got fed up with refilling his fountain pen, put his head together with brother Georg and patented the ballpoint. Except not quite so happy, as various patent struggles broke out shortly after World War Two (when early Biro models served in the RAF). They were essentially won by a Frenchman, Baron Marcel Bich (subtract the 'h' — you've got it) and the Parker® company.

Even less simple, in Croatia, Eduard Slavoljub Penkala (1871–1922) is hailed as the inventor of the ballpoint and a Biro is called a 'Penkala'. Extremists even claim that the word 'pen' comes from his name, although more orthodox sources derive it from Latin *penna* or feather. Croatian national hero Penkala, by the way, was born in Slovakia to a Polish father and a Dutch mother, but let's not get into that or any other Balkan arguments. In any case, the very first (commercially unexploited and then forgotten) patent for a ballpoint was taken out by American John J. Loud in 1888.

MORE

At any branch of **W.H.Smith**

Derivation of pen:

www.etymonline.com/p4etym.htm

Another theory

www.croatiaemb.org/C_U_relations/Cro&USA/part12.htm

the **biggest** company in the field:

www.bicworld.com/

'Ball point art', make of it what you will:

groups.msn.com/ballpointpenart/_homepage.msnw?pgmarket=en-us

Brassaï

Brassó, Transylvania, Hungary (Now Bra°ov, Romania) 1899– 984 Eze, France

Photographer and nighthawk

'When you meet the man you see at once that he's equipped with no ordinary eyes' —

Henry Miller

Brassaï, born Halász Gyula, uncovered in a series of startling photo-monographs the unexplored and taboo life of Paris. The essential great metropolis of the nineteenth century, with its iron bridges, decorated glass and machine brick, is revealed in its maturity as an organism that reproduces many of its pleasures and necessities nocturnally. With classic immigrant risk-taking and panache Brassaï daringly butted his nose (and his camera) into mobster bars up at the Goutte d'Or district, spied at police on the graveyard shift having a quiet fag outside their ramshackle station in the fifth arrondissement, and even, notoriously, managed to photograph employees in the *apartées* of Paris brothels or posing for their clients in negligées.

Other kinds of previously unacknowledged behaviour were carefully documented too: the lesbian haunt of Le Monocle, with its carefully jacketed dykes and simpering fems, the inter-racial *bal nègre* in the Rue Blomet, with its musclely African studs; or the simple dancehall *bals musettes* of the near suburbs, where proletarians drank and coupled-up. Brassaï and his fellow nighthawks realized the significance of the so-called ephemeral in the construction of a civilization's pleasures and needs.

Brassaï was not working in isolation. His companions of the night were writers and poets like Jacques Prévert, Henry Miller and Raymond Queneau, Surrealist and Bohemian experimenters and explorers in the jungles of subconscious desire. Like the Pole Joseph Conrad, who brought a detached, sardonic and daring eye to the machinery of empire in his famous novella *Heart of Darkness*, they all pursued the everyday into the everynight, turned over the stone casually passed by to reveal all that swarmed beneath it.

It's unsurprising that one of the founders of the modernist visual sensibility was a Central European, a displaced Transylvanian, a poor immigrant in Paris, on the edge of its social and economic life until, by throwing some light on its outer darkness, he steps into the light himself as one of the most celebrated and daring photographers of his age.

MORE

Books:

Brassaï - The Monograph Alain Sayag and Annick Lionel-Marie (2000)

Henry Miller, Happy Rock. Brassaï (2002)

The whole **Henry Miller/ Brassaï saga** in books at:

www.google.co.uk/search?sourceid=navclient&ie=UTF-8&oe=UTF-8&q=Miller+on+Brassai

Many of Brassai's great **photographs** can be seen on the web: Google 'Brassai' as an image search

Or **look** at:

www.masters-of-photography.com/B/brassai/brassai.html

George Buday

Kolozsvár, Transylvania, Hungary (now Cluj-Napoca, Romania) 1907–1990 London, England

Cultural activist and illustrator

Senki sem próféta a saját, maga hazájában (Nobody is a prophet in his own country)

Starting in his youth in Transylvania, (from 1920 a part of Romania with a large Hungarian population), Buday worked to encourage local cultural life, eventually moving to Szeged in Hungary to study and to organize a theatre festival. From then on he worked on innumerable woodcut illustrations for books, including ballad collections, Shakespeare's *The Tempest*, François Mauriac's *Life of Jesus* and *The Rubáiyát of Omar Khayyám*. He also fitted in a study of housing conditions in the Britain and tried to apply what he'd learnt back home. Returning to Britain in 1939, he worked for the BBC's Hungarian service and so the Nazi-friendly Hungarian government of the period deprived him of his citizenship. He was briefly back in favour during the democratic interlude of 1945-9, and headed up the official Hungarian Cultural Institute in London. When the wind started to blow from Moscow in 1949 and cultural exchange with the 'decadent west' was no longer required, the Institute was shut down.

Buday beavered on with his art and became a leading British illustrator in a period when illustration flourished. He extended his activities to producing the definitive work on the British Christmas card. He was undoubtedly an exemplary man, idealist, artist, activist — but the news of the cruel defeat of the 1956 uprising in Hungary brought on a grave nervous breakdown and he was confined to a mental hospital. The fate and the suffering of George Buday illustrates the destiny of many of Hungary's most creative and dynamic figures in the twentieth century.

The good news though is firstly, that he managed to continue to work even in hospital, and, secondly, that Hungary once more has a Cultural Centre in London, headed by another energetic and polymathic personality, Katalin Bogyay.

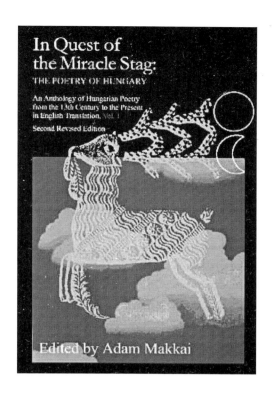

MORE

Books:

The History of the Christmas Card George Buday (1954 re-issued 1992)

Arabian Fairy Tales, retold by Amina Shah, with wood-engravings by George Buday (1969)

Life of Jesus François Mauriac, illustrated by George Buday (1937)

In Quest of the Miracle Stag The Poetry of Hungary , Ed. by Adam Makkai and Illustrated by George Buday (1996)

Hungarian Cultural Centre, 10 Maiden Lane, London WC2E 7NA

tel. 0207 240 8448 fax 0207 240 4847 culture@hungary.org.uk
www.hungary.org.uk

Robert Capa

Budapest, Hungary 1913–1954 Thai Binh, Vietnam

Photojournalist

'The Greatest War Photographer in the World: Robert Capa' — *Picture Post*

While Hungarian émigré photographer Brassaï was uncovering the seamy nocturnal *imaginaire* of Paris Capital of the Nineteenth Century, (as Walter Benjamin named it), another brilliant and bold Hungarian snapper was producing a similarly revealing and eventually defining vision of modern war. It was Capa who supplied one of the two most famous images of twentieth-century war, the white-clothed Spanish *miliciano* at the moment of death, head jerked back, rifle falling from his hand — the classic picture of the ordinary man and soldier caught in the political game of war. The other image must be Nick Ut's photograph of the naked 9-year-old Vietnamese girl Kim Phuc, fleeing down a road from her napalmed village — the parallel image of the civilian and non-uniformed victim of war, the twentieth-century's terrifying military accomplishment, of spreading war to the dwellings of the enemy, his wife and kids.

This development was signalled by one of Capa's 'campaigns', the Spanish Civil War, which brought aerial destruction of the undefended ancient city of Guernica by German bombers in 1937.

Capa was influenced by the leftist cultural and political ferment of interwar Hungary, adopting some of his attitudes about photography from the social documentarist *Szociofotó* movement before he emigrated to Paris. The war he captured in Spain, China, the D-Day landings, Israel and Vietnam (where he was killed by a mine) is the war of ordinary grunts and ragged refugees, moving, heart-rending, rarely heroic.

Capa was hard-drinking, aggressive, handsome, daring and seductive. His biography is about to be 'Hollywoodized' in a film starring Pierce Brosnan, an actor who has played James Bond 007. Will today's bland cinematic production line manage to evoke such a mixture of despair, humanity and talent as Capa possessed?

MORE
Pierce Brosnan will soon portray Robert Capa in a **film** *Blood and Champagne*

Books:

Blood and Champagne: The Life and Times of Robert Capa Alex Kershaw (2001)

Heart of Spain Robert Capa's Photographs of the Spanish Civil War (2003)

Robert Capa: The Definitive Collection Ed. Richard Whelan (2001)

Websites with images about Capa:

www.pbs.org/wnet/americanmasters/database/capa_r.html

home.planet.nl/%7Emonique.schilders/europe/capa3.html

The photo that **made Capa's name:**

www.users.cloud9.net/~bradmcc/ trotsky.html

More on **Kim Phuc** and Nick Ut's famous Vietnam photo

www.cbc.ca/news/indepth/kimphuc/

André Deutsch

Budapest, Hungary 1917–2000 London, England

Entrepreneur of the imagination

Megfogta az Isten lábát (He has caught the leg of God)

Before it became swamped by giant corporations that occupy literary space with derivative, unchallenging 'products' backed by massive promotional spends, British Book Publishing was an arena for innovation and for quirky, headstrong figures like the Central Europeans André Deutsch (Hungary) and George Weidenfeld (Austria), Victor Gollancz with his Polish background, and Allen Lane, the founder of Penguin Books and inventor of the quality mass paperback. Deutsch was, as another legendary independent publisher John Calder put it, an 'entrepreneur of the imagination'. Calder was reflecting on a career that began when the young André Deutsch, escaping *Anschluss* Austria where he was finishing his education, discovered publishing in an internment camp for enemy aliens on the Isle of Man.

With the help of a talented ex-lover, Diana Athill, he set up two separate publishing ventures after the war, one of them the eponymous André Deutsch imprint. He went on to make his name with titles originally written in German, where he had the advantage of a fluency lacking in most of his rivals' editorial offices. When the fascination with the defeated enemy waned, he astutely connected with a golden age of postwar American fiction by publishing Norman Mailer, Jack Kerouac, John Updike and Philip Roth, as well as putting into print significant women writers like Stevie Smith, Margaret Atwood and Jean Rhys. A keen appreciation of British life and obsessions inspired him to commission his compatriot George Mikes's wildly successful unpicking of the national knot, *How To Be An Alien*, as well as successful series on cricket, Scotch whisky and other Britannic arcana.

What an extraordinary contrast André Deutsch, with his cosmopolitan daring, makes to the publishing executives of today, endlessly chasing the 'next' Bridget Jones, Harry Potter or celebrity cook/hairdresser/cosmetic surgeon/footie hero with a juicy TV tie-in. To this crowd, the idea of books as a source of intellectual diversity and challenge, well you might as well be speaking Hungarian…. Hopefully we won't have to wait for another European conflagration before we get a breath of fresh air through their fetid counting houses.

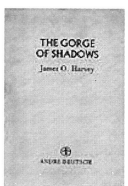

MORE
Obsessions of Britain's booktrade today see
The Bookseller at your local library or on the web:
www.thebookseller.com
Stet **Diana Athill** (2000)
The André Deutsch **archive:**
www.lib.utulsa.edu/speccoll/deutsa00.htm
The André Deutsch **collection:**
www.brookes.ac.uk/services/library/speccoll/deutsch.html

Tibor Fischer
Stockport, England 1959–
Novelist

A béka feneke alatt van (Under the frog's arse)* — Hungarian saying

While 1960s and 1970s Britain saw what one could almost call a 'genre' of Cold War novels, plays, *samizdat* translations and other literary reports 'from behind the curtain', sometimes tragic, often sarcastic in tone — one thinks of Solzhenitsyn, Milan Kundera, Christa Wolf and Tadeusz Borowski — by the 1980s the genre was dissolving as fast as the 'really existing socialism'** it comments on. It could be said to have ended with the aptly titled *Poland under Black Light* by Janusz Anderman published in 1985.

A sort of postscript to this genre, and quite strangely distinct from post-collapse narratives like Victor Pelevin's *Russian Disco,* is the 'second generation' voice of Tibor Fischer, the son of a Hungarian émigré. Fischer grew up in England, but evidently absorbed a good deal of background and anecdotes from his parents' experience of Hungary.

Just how much was demonstrated by the rather unlikely literary success of his first book *Under the Frog* (1992), an ironical, picaresque look at Hungary from 1944 to 1956, through the lives of a team of young basketball players on tour, in training and so on. The material is derived, Fischer tells us, from talking to his parents, both professional players before they emigrated in 1956, and from his own stay in Hungary as a journalist during the period 1988–90. It is interesting to compare *Under the Frog* with works written by 'real' Hungarians, because Fischer's is a very (very English?) distanced and humorous regard — life as prolonged joke — that seems like the rictus of tragedy. There is the sadness and cynicism of events themselves. Here is just one example: a competitive examination and new peasant 'cadres' have been given the answers to their maths questions in advance, so their promotion is not in doubt, as the regime has decreed the need for a new 'toiling intelligentsia' to replace the educated class of the past. There is also, no doubt, the sadness of having to live all this at secondhand, being brought up in a Hungarian bubble in England.

Fischer's subsequent books have been set in France and South London, but he still plays an important role as a reviewer and in appearing at Hungarian-themed events in Britain.

The Fischer saga, man and book, tells us something about the great peculiarity of the divided Europe of his Cold War generation — how cut off one half was from the other. Possibly we in the West were more cut off from them than vice-versa. East Germans turned their TV antennas west, books and records were smuggled in, copied and traded all over the Eastern Bloc. But cultural influence the other way was limited to visits by the Moscow State Circus (or the Red Army Choir if you lucked out totally) and one visit by Bertholt Brecht's Berliner Ensemble in 1956 (which interestingly enough revolutionized British theatre for the next twenty-five years...).

*i.e. a place from where you can sink no deeper

**a phrase once current that used to mean 'not that wispy pie-in-the-sky socialism of idealists, utopians and social democrats, but real down-to-earth boot-in-your-face good old Uncle Joe Stalinism.'

MORE

Tibor Fischer **reviews** Hungary:

books.guardian.co.uk/review/story/0,12084,908957,00.html

later books by Tibor Fischer:

The Thought Gang (1994)

The Collector Collector (1997)

Don't Read This Book If You're Stupid (2000)

Voyage to the End of the Room (2003)

The **British Council's** profile of Fischer:

www.contemporarywriters.com/authors/?p=auth35

a **good** interview:

webdoc.gwdg.de/edoc/ia/eese/artic97/bayer/9_97.html

(also available as a **sound file!**)

That **Brecht visit:**

observer.guardian.co.uk/uk_news/story/0,6903,582184,00.html

Eugene Fodor

Léva, Hungary (now Levice, Slovakia) 1905–1991 Litchfield, Connecticut, USA

Guidebook pioneer

Ahány ház, annyi szokás (So many houses, so many customs)

Eugene Fodor was a major innovator of mass tourism thanks to his intelligent and well-produced guidebooks, written with an emphasis that was broadcast in the title of the very first guide, the best-selling progenitor of a now huge series, *1936 — On the Continent. The Entertaining Travel Annual.* Fodor was addressing a new middle-class constituency of travellers seeking 'the happy thrill that foreign travel ought to give you'. This was not the stodgy travel-as-improvement model assumed in Baedeker and its worthy imitators, but something more lighthearted.

In retrospect, the Europe of 1936 was hardly an innocent's playground, although Fodor's team of writers (with an endearingly large cast of fellow-Hungarians including the novelist Lajos Zihaly) tried to steer around this. The 1936 guide to Spain — then being ripped apart by a bloody Civil War — refers in reality to the more tranquil 1935 version of the country (when of course the book was written). In Germany, 'since the change of government' the country was 'definitely attaining' a greater national unity; and on a train, the author notes a 'particularly fine-looking fair man, wearing a really very well cut black uniform over his brown shirt, indicating that he was a high official in the S.S.'. Fodor's thrill-seeking envoy notices rather a lot of uniforms about, but puts this down to a quirky German 'national characteristic' — perhaps today he might see it as gene-determined behaviour. Later Hitler himself pops up as potentially quite a worthy cove 'a great music lover' who has also 'personally designed the interior' of the Nazi HQ in Munich, the Brown House.

MORE
Shock horror!
J.G.Ballard *High Rise* (1975)

Ernő Goldfinger (Riba Drawings Monograph Series No 3) Robert Elwall (2003)

Famous buildings:
2 Willow Road, Hampstead, London NW3:
www.nationaltrust.org.uk
Trellick Tower, 5 Golborne Road W10, near Westbourne Park underground station (just look up!)
Haggerston Girls School Weymouth Terrace, Hackney, E2

New biography
Ernő Goldfinger: The Life of an Architect Nigel Warburton (2003)

Harry Houdini

Budapest, Hungary 1874–1926 Detroit, Michigan

Escapologist and celebrity prototype

Minden csoda három napig tart (Every wonder lasts three days)

Houdini was one of the most famous Hungarians of the modern age. But his story is archetypically an American story, or should that be a Jewish story? He didn't just escape from locked chests, chains, underwater tanks and hanging mid-air in a straitjacket, he also escaped from being Hungarian by claiming Appleton, Wisconsin as his birthplace and from being Jewish by changing his birthname 'Erik Weisz' to the Italian-American sounding Harry Houdini. He also disguised his Rabbi father as the religiously ambiguous 'Reverend Doctor Mayer'.

Unskilled and uneducated Harry Houdini escaped from a life of hard graft into an early version of showbiz celebrity. He spiced up his act considerably — using the excuse that the audience must be sure he was not concealing cutting tools about his person — by emerging from his artificial confinements nude. In fact he seems to have escaped from almost all the constraints the nineteenth century had in store for a poor immigrant boy.

His is a classic showbiz outsider's story. His stunts were effortful, painful, ultimately dull and overwhelmingly pointless, but his massive celebrity became the attraction in itself. He was a cultural symbol, a hero, for the cultureless immigrant masses of America, then of London, Paris, Berlin. A jealous stalker ended his life by punching him ferociously in the stomach and rupturing his appendix.

Houdini was a magnificent precursor of the anodyne and simplistic American pop culture, his audiences created by mass advertising and theatre promoters. Don't ask what it is you've paid to see (a man emerging from a doorway essentially) you've seen the celebrated Harry Houdini!

What is less well-known is that Houdini became a bitter public opponent of spiritualism and its money-spinning mediums after Arthur Conan Doyle's wife 'spoke' using Houdini's dead mother's voice at a séance, but using a cut-glass English accent and not *di mama's* broken Yiddish, as Harry couldn't help but point out.

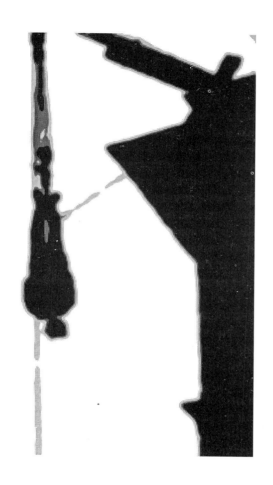

MORE

Harry speaks:

Miracle Mongers And Their Methods H.Houdini (1920)

An informative site for a **documentary** film on Houdini:

www.pbs.org/wgbh/amex/houdini/filmmore/transcript/index.html

Attila József

Budapest, Hungary 1905–1937 Balatonszárszó, Hungary

Poet and working-class hero (real one)

'My leader is in my heart' — József ('A breath of air')

John Lennon, considered by some to be a poet, famously sang about being a 'working-class hero'. He actually came from the right side of the tracks and was to enjoy a tremendously wealthy (and isolated) lifestyle, despite the radical posing and the lamentable records made with Yoko. In Attila József, by contrast, we have one of Hungary's most admired poets, who brilliantly fused folk tradition and modernism and genuinely was the son of a washerwoman who died of overwork. His own attempt to escape penury as a schoolteacher failed because of his radical opinions and notoriety in a then highly conservative country.

Rather than trying out meditation or designer drugs in the back of limos, József was fated to sell newspapers outdoors in Budapest and Vienna. In his own words: 'I have been a tutor, newspaper vendor, ship's boy, stenographer, typist, guard in a cornfield, poet, translator, critic, busboy, stevedore, construction worker, day labourer' ('C.V.', from *Selected poems and texts*).

Unsurprisingly, his verse was often raw, angry, spiritually violent. In his famous 'With a Pure Heart' he wrote: 'I have no father and no mother/ I have no country and god.../ for three days now I didn't eat/ not even a piece of bread.../ with a pure heart, I'll burn and loot/if I have to, I'll even shoot.' Looking at Europe in the mid-1930s, he saw rather accurately: 'O Europe is so many borders/ on every border murderers' ('O Europe'). And in the year Hitler was acclaimed to power by the German *Volk*: 'My leader is in my heart./ We are men, not beasts,/ We have minds. While our hearts ripen desires,/ they cannot be kept in files./ Come, freedom! Give birth to a new order,/ teach me with good words and let me play,/ your beautiful serene son.' (from 'A breath of air').

Yet József wrote many tender fugues too, as in 'Since You've been Away': 'I thought I was in a mild valley,/ protected north and south by your breasts,/ where dawn flowers in my hair/ and evening shines upon my feet...

If only John Lennon had paid his dues selling newspapers or guarding a cornfield, and Attila József had had three good meals per diem and a doting Japanese wife. In the end, József threw himself under a train, attacked by both Right and Left, a sufferer from 'schizoid tendencies', but also one who lived that 'schizophrenia' of class-crossing, the woodchopper poet, son of the washerwoman, trying to breathe the air of literature, a world made for and by the gentry.

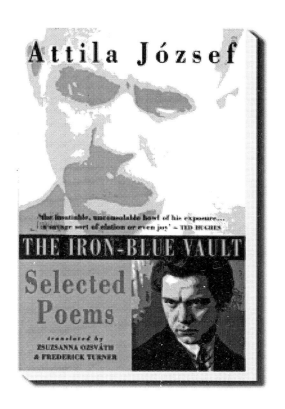

MORE

The József **citations** in the text all come from John Bátkti's translations:
'A Breath of Air!' translated by John Bátkti and L.Hyde is at:
www.humanbeams.com/pagebreak/pb03Jozsef-breathofair.html
Selected poems and texts tr. John Bátki, ed. by George Gömöri and James Atlas (1973)
Winter night: selected poems of Attila József tr. John Bátki (1998)
Also
Poems Ed. Thomas Kabdebo; tr. Michael Beevor et al (1966)
Poems and fragments tr. John Bátki et al. edited and introduced by Thomas Kabdebo foreword by Peter Denman with an essay on the poetry of Attila József by Miklós Szabolcsi (1999)
The Iron-Blue Vault : selected poems tr.Zsuzsanna Ozsváth and Frederick Turner. (1999)

Imre Kertész

Budapest, Hungary 1929–

Nobel laureate and literary radical

Bedobták a mélyvízbe (To be thrown in at the deep end) — Hungarian saying

Just as the war years turned Imre Kertész's life upside down, so he turned the form of the novel, and the 'Holocaust novel' in particular upside down. His highly unusual masterpiece *Fateless* largely dispenses with characters, narrative development and psychology — all the familiar props of the novel-writing business. The horrors of parental and then personal deportation, the selection ramp, the 'showers' where those who SS doctors decided were not even worth working to death were rapidly murdered: all these are matter-of-factly, coolly, detachedly noted.

Like Primo Levi's *Moments of Reprieve* and *The Drowned and the Saved*, this is a 'survivor' account. But crucially, Kertész passed through Auschwitz and Buchenwald as an adolescent. *Fateless* begins with typical adolescent awkwardness at his father's show of feeling as he leaves for forced labour service, in a hurry and possibly for ever. From this moment on we share the distancing and only partly comprehending perspective of a youngster in the highly organized human turmoil of the camps. His diffidence and incomprehension are the threads that draw us into a sense of what went on in those places. Writing years after the events, Kertész has created an immediacy of experience in his attempt to bridge what he sensed in 1945 was the enormous chasm that exists between those who experienced the camps and the rest of us: the Germans' great crime is protected from being truly perceived in its ghastly magnitude by its very horror. Even the highly allusive way in which Kertész treats it creates a shudder: 'I noticed some blue lines on his wrist, numbers from Auschwitz. His number was in the millions' (*Fateless*, p161).

Fateless was initially received without acclaim in Hungary. It was followed by *Kaddish for a Child Unborn* in which Kertész strips away even more of the novelistic equipment and addresses us directly, involves us in his inner monologue about Auschwitz and its consequences. Here, though, we're being addressed by an adult, a man who has lived more than the camps, has been married, lived, loved. Yet he needs to speak to us about what he feels the lessons of Auschwitz might be, to let us try and learn something from this supreme human débâcle. One proposal he makes is an interesting 'upside-down' definition of freedom; doing precisely the thing you aren't obliged to do, as when a camp inmate receives another's ration by mistake and, under no obligation but the personal choice to make a moral act, passes it over to him — a real moment of will and decision for a starving man. Freedom clawed from the grip of extreme adversity. Even in the narrowest sphere of action, Kertész informs us, one can still act with humanity and dignity — as was revealed to him under the desperate night-time glow of Auschwitz.

MORE

Interview with Kertesz and his **Nobel** acceptance speech:

www.nobel.se/literature/laureates/2002/kertesz-interview.htm

Translations:

Fateless, tr. Christopher C. Wilson and Katharina M. Wilson (1992)

Kaddish for a Child not Born, tr. Christopher C. Wilson and Katharina M. Wilson (1997)

Kincsem the Horse

Tapiószentmárton, Hungary 1874–1887

Champion racing filly

'The Hungarian miracle' (*Sporting Life*)

A splendid and heroic creature, a Hungarochamp, here in her own magnificent right as 'the world's most successful horse' (*Guinness Book of Records*). She entered fifty-four races, including the highly select Goodwood, and won every single one of them. We also include her among our Eminent Hungarians as a reminder that Hungary and the rest of the world are not yet solely a landscape of human beings, but also the living space of our fabulous friends, helpers, entertainers and co-beings, especially the equine, canine and feline races that make our lives bearable and possible.

This particular member of the equine race was extraordinary enough to have various websites and a hotel (in 'Kincsem country') dedicated to her memory — not bad for a hoss who passed on to hoss heaven over a hundred years ago. But more than an equestrian champion, she was also a character, often quietly standing at the start to munch on grass well after the race had begun to give her competitors an interesting lead — which of course she always stole back! Kincsem the wonder-mare conquered the Turf of Europe by rail, racing in Britain, Austria, France and Germany. She would travel only with her favourite groom, Frankie, and her personal companion, a cat. If neither was present she simply wouldn't get inside her rail truck. And once abroad she would sup only on oats brought from her stud farm and water from its spring.

Kincsem left five foals, Budagyöngye, Olyan-Nincs, Talpra Magyar, Kincs-Őr and Kincs, to continue her bloodline into posterity. Her descendants race successfully to this day.

She was, and is, the pride of Hungary. Whisper it softly, many of her antecedents were British horses, but she was certainly bred in a beautiful part of Hungary, also home to the Ászár wines such as Ezerjó, Szürkebarát and Ászári Asszonyfektető. Ask for them at your local off licence!*

*Hungarian pronunciation guide: www.star.net.nz/magyar.htm

** a small site about Hungarian wine with wonderful landscape pictures

www.fsz.bme.hu/hungary/cuisine/drinks/wines.html

MORE:

More on Hungarian wine at:

www.winesofhungary.com/regions.htm

The **standard** source on Kincsem (but in Hungarian only):

KINCSEM a Magyar Csoda (The Hungarian Wonder) Dr. Fehér Dezső (1998)

A **good site** in German:

www.kincsem.de/pferde/kincsem.htm

A **hotel** in 'Kincsem Country':

www.kincsemhotel.hu/programokeng.html

Kincsem **horse park**:

www.cyberius.hu/fogathajtovb/kincsem_en.htm

Check the **stud book**, Kincsem's complete pedigree is at:

www.thoroughbredchampions.com/gallery/kincsem.htm

Zoltán Kodály

Kecskemét, Hungary 1882–1967 Budapest, Hungary

Composer and anti-globalization activist

A jó pap holtig tanul (A good priest learns until his death)

Kodály (like Béla Bartók) collected Hungarian folk songs and also produced a huge opus of choral pieces, working, especially with the country's two communist regimes (in 1919 and after 1948), to organize mass musical participation via the choral tradition. He earnestly lived out his two-fold mission of preserving local musical traditions — personally collecting over 5,000 tunes in 235 villages — and opening up musical participation. In his own words: 'Music is an indispensable part of universal human knowledge'. Music should belong to everyone… There are regions of the human soul which can be illuminated only through music.' Ideas that seem both to at the same time chime with the Marxist régimes that sponsored his work in their notion of cultural popularizing, and to point at a human complexity well beyond the dreams of Socialist Realism and the latest pig-iron figures.

Coming from a modest social background, Kodály based his theory of musical education on the one instrument accessible to all, the human voice, and thought musical training should proceed naturally from working with the local song tradition. His Hungary certainly had this tradition in abundance, although when he started collecting at the turn of the twentieth century, it was disappearing under the impact of both the German language and of professionally written songs.

Kodály was an early and sophisticated opponent of the kind of globalization of popular culture that causes the impoverishing loss of local cultural knowledge. Yet more than this, his present relevance derives from his effective interest in how people can connect with their cultural traditions and be active cultural participators rather than mere consumers. Since Kodály's birth we have progressed through printed sheet music, mass-produced pianos and the shellac record to individual mp3 players and a centralized music business that attempts to drown out, in popular music, anything but adolescent (or should that be pre-teen?) tastes and themes. Today, given the instant global reach and economic power of the culture corporations, and their homogenous mass products, all of the world's local cultures are threatened in the same way as Kodály perceived his beloved Magyar tradition being threatened one hundred years ago.

MORE

Major choral works include the sombre but inspiring *Missa Brevis*, penned in the depths of World War Two. and the *Psalmus Hungaricus*.

For **instrumental music** listen to the sparkling *Harry Janos Suite* and the *Duo for Violin and Cello, Op.7,* which exploits the bareness and sophistication of this pairing with the lightness and energy of folk inspiration

On the **Kodály method** of musical education follow the worldwide links on: www.kodaly-inst.hu/links.htm

Arthur Koestler

Budapest, Hungary 1905–1983 London, England

Prophet or Prat?

Szemesnek áll a világ (The world waits on him who sees)

As an enthusiastic communist in the 1930s, Koestler discovered that Joseph Stalin was the true inspiration of all subjected mankind. After five years of Party loyalty he made a further discovery — the OGPU* were really up to no good. Turning himself into a historian he 'discovered' that the European Jews were really 'Khazars' (an Asiatic tribal confederation around in the Dark Ages) rather than the Children of Father Abraham as they like to think. A further and late Koestler discovery was that there really *are* pixies at the bottom of the garden and he endowed a chair of Paraphysics (at Edinburgh University), hoping to disseminate this and allied notions.

Where to start with this curious and once extremely famous figure? His father Henrik Koestler invented radioactive soap (which hasn't stayed the course for some reason). Very much a journalist at heart, Koestler loved to be where the action was: throwing up his university studies to work with Zionist pioneers in 1920s Palestine; becoming a journalist in Berlin in 1930; flying over the North Pole in a Zeppelin in 1931; writing for an anti-Hitler paper in Paris after 1933; reporting the Spanish Civil War in 1936 and 1937; moving to an embattled England in the 1940s; visiting the newly independent Israel in 1948 and so on. After earning world renown with his novel *Darkness at Noon* (1940), based on the Stalinist madness of the Moscow Trials, he progressed to writing about science *The Sleepwalkers* (1959) and philosophy, archeology and religion *The Yogi and the Commissar* (1945).

Koestler was an admirably polymathic figure, especially compared to today's arid academic specialists or celebrity-obsessed journos. Unfortunately one of his best-known books today is *The Thirteenth Tribe* (1976) which anti-Semites of the European or Palestinian-Fundamentalist persuasion twist to 'illuminate' their particular nasty kettles of fish. Magyar maven Peter Sherwood sees the 'discovery' of the Khazars as part of Koestler's long-standing attempt to escape the confines of his ethnicity: the historically vague and Asiatic Khazars can, give or take a leap in the dark or two, be construed as kinsmen of the Magyars (or some of them). Perhaps Koestler should have finished that degree course after all.

On the other hand nobody has excelled Arthur Koestler's guilt-ridden self-examination of his own delusion. For instance he confessed that while visiting the Ukraine in Party-loyal mode in 1932, he witnessed 'crowds of begging families' at the railway stations, as a Soviet-induced famine swept away millions yet he persuaded himself this was all 'the heritage of the past'.

Perhaps this story is still relevant: even as Communism has lost its mule-like kick to the brains of some of the most intelligent of people it seems to have been replaced by certain other enthusiasms of a similarly ruthless nature.

*a predecessor of the KGB, the Soviet secret police

MORE

David Cesarani's recent **biography:**

Arthur Koestler The Homeless Mind (1998) sees Koestler as a déraciné intellectual with a problem about his heritage, (possibly inherited from his snooty Viennese mama) and, fashionably enough, delves into Koestler's excessively macho treatment of the fairer sex.

From the thirty-nine 'major works' Cesarani cites *The Sleepwalkers* (1959) and *Darkness at Noon* (1940) as amongst his most resilient.

Some Koestler **quotes:**

orwell.ru/people/koestler

Joseph Kosma

Budapest, Hungary 1905–1969 La Roche-Guyon, France

Composer of 'Autumn Leaves'

En ce temps-là, la vie était plus belle
Et le soleil plus brûlant qu'aujourd'hui
Tu étais ma plus douce amie
Mais je n'ai que faire des regrets

> — *Les Feuilles mortes* ('Autumn Leaves') with words by Jacques Prévert and
> music by Joseph Kosma

The career of Joseph Kosma (and that of his cinematic collaborators, director Marcel Carné and scriptwriter-lyricist Jacques Prévert) demonstrates the heights that European cinema reached before TV and Hollywood became the dominant models for its film-makers. This particular triumvirate created several wonders in a golden age of French cinema that gave birth to *Les Enfants du Paradis*, perhaps the most celebrated French film ever made, and Kosma also wrote film scores for films of the great director Jean Renoir including *La Vie est à nous, La Règle du jeu* (1939) and *French Cancan* (1955).

But the particular wonder that marks the peak of their acheivement, the film in which the famous and much-recorded song *Les Feuilles Mortes* or 'Autumn Leaves' was first heard was *Les Portes de la Nuit (The Gates of the Night)* (1946). Made just after France had re-entered the daylight after the sordid era of the Occupation, its ambiguous and tense, dark and foggy tone expresses perfectly what is still a very obscured period in the nation's history. *Les Portes de la Nuit* is a story of betrayal and incipient revenge that captures a mood of impotent anger and sadness. A young working-class Resistance fighter (Yves Montand) is told by an unearthly and prophetic tramp that he is fated to encounter the most beautiful woman in the world. She indeed appears on the scene and his joy is boundless. But it turns out that it was her brother who betrayed him to the Gestapo. Archetypes of beauty, mysterious wisdom, innocence, suffering and evil — all as in a dream. In the France of 1946 the Liberation must have seemed like a dream and the Occupation a recent nightmare. Except, except it was all horribly real and its crimes — a still widely unpalatable truth — were committed by Frenchmen as well as Germans.

As many artists have found, in the face of immense tragedy and disgrace only a symbolic, 'mythical' representation allows us the emotional fluidity and space to try to encompass them. This is the technique of the oblique, mysterious *Les Portes de la Nuit* and of Kosma's splendid and haunting song.

MORE

That movie:

Les Portes de la Nuit (in French) for •17.46:

www.alapage.com/mx/?tp=F&type=4&VID_NUMERO=328240

Sheet music for Autumn Leaves:

www.laurasmidi.com/cgi-bin/ shmtitles.cgi?newtitle=Autumn%20Leaves

A **formal** version:

www.iclassics.com/iclassics/album.jsp?selectionId=3420

A **Jazz** version (with a sample):

http://mfile.akamai.com/6560/wm2/muze.download.akamai.com/2890/us/
uswm2/393/498393_1_01.asx?obj=v30923

Book on Kosma:

Joseph Kosma, 1905-1969. un homme, un musicien Maurice Fleuret (1989)

Lajos Kossuth

Monok, Hungary 1802–1894 Turin, Italy

Hungarian patriot and International Democratic Hero

'Who is the man to whom all nations pay a tribute of respect such as no material power can command, poor outcast though he was?' — Count Albert Apponyi

The Kossuth story is one of those Hungarian tragedies where the outer tragedy masks another, deeper, one. Kossuth, a brilliant lawyer, orator and journalist, descended from an enlightened Protestant wing of the Hungarian nobility, led a national revolt against the Habsburg-ruled Austrian Empire. His breakaway Hungarian Republic, which was eventually to enact extremely advanced legislation, including the emancipation of the Jews, came up against the resistance of the emperor in Vienna, who called in the armies of his ally the Russian czar. Independent Hungary was crushed after less than two years. For many inside and outside the country — he made extensive and well-received speaking tours in England, France and the U.S.A. — Kossuth was the 'Apostle of Liberty', a Central European Garibaldi and 'The George Washington of Europe' to the Americans.

Behind the tragic defeat of the first Hungarian Republic lay the greater tragedy of the breakdown of national cohabitation. National independence for Hungary, then a land with substantial minorities (ethnic Hungarians made up only 48 per cent of the population) — Slovak, Croat, Romanian in particular — meant, initially at least, a blunt rejection of the national claims of these other peoples. 'All men are created equal but some are created more Hungarian than others', to borrow from Orwell. Even if by the end of the War of Independence the Hungarian legislature began to change its attitude to the different nationalities, the damage had been done.

Kossuth was undoubtedly and justifiably a national and international hero. But at the same time, this was also the period in which the Pandora's box of Central European nationalism was opened.

Nowadays we might note that, eagerly promoted by a certain Dr Otto von Habsburg MEP, the newly enlarged European Union is recreating many of the positive aspects of the old Empire — a multinational trading bloc and federation of different peoples — that were destroyed by the creation of new states and borders following its collapse in 1918.

MORE

Hear the great man's voice at:

hungary.ciw.edu/kossuth/voice.html

In his own words:

Memories of my Exile Lajos Kossuth (1880)

A major recent **re-examination** of his legacy

The Lawful Revolution: Louis Kossuth and the Hungarians, 1848-1849 I. Deak (1979)

Read Count Apponyi's moving eulogy to Kossuth at the invaluable 'Bartleby' site:

www.bartleby.com/268/7/51.html

Kossuth **wows** America:

hipcat.hungary.org/users/hipcat/kossuth.htm

György Kurtág
Lugoj, Romania 1926–

Composer and teacher

"No no no no no no no no!" (Kurtág to a piano student)

The eventual international success of György Kurtág as a contemporary composer demonstrates that cultural life in communist Hungary was, especially after 1956, much more complex that a simplistic 'Soviet traffic-light model' (red-red-red) suggests. Earlier, between 1949 and 1953, even some of Béla Bartók's work had been banned and not a note of Schoenberg could be heard until 1955. It was generally extremely difficult to get access to 'new music', through performance, sheet music or records. Kurtág, who had decided he wanted to compose at the age of thirteen after hearing Schubert's *Unfinished Symphony* on the radio, crossed over into Hungary from Romania hoping to study with Bartók himself, although the master's early death prevented this.

Later Kurtág had the opportunity to travel abroad and studied in Paris with Darius Milhaud and Olivier Messiaen. He subsequently returned to Hungary where he developed — slowly — his own work, at pains to employ only the most minimal of elements and equipment, possibly, as Rachel Beckles Willson suggests in the excellent *Central European Review*, as a reaction, 'a process necessary, perhaps, [for someone] who had suffered a dictatorship's indoctrination with extravagant, vacuous, rhetorical slogans'.*

Kurtág has spent many years as a noted teacher, as a *répetiteur* for younger musicians. Eventually this led him to compose a series of 'Games' for piano — he says he only understands music when he teaches it. Here is the same democratic principle that motivates so many of the Hungarians who have contributed to cultural understanding and appreciation in the widest sense, including Kodály, Pető and Lábán. Other work by Kurtág derives from a fascinated engagement with both events of everyday life, like the song-elegy *Gravestone for Stephan* written in 1979 in memory of a former teacher, and with the sound-shapes of the Russian language which, according to Rachel Beckles Willson, he learnt especially in order to read Dostoevsky and that led to the compositions *Messages of the Late Miss R V Troussova op 17* (1976-1980) and the *Songs of Despair and Sorrow op 18* (1980-1994).

*The Mind is a Free Creature. The music of György Kurtág' by Rachel Beckles Willson: www.ce-review.org/00/12/willson12.html

KURTÁG

JÁTÉKOK
SPIELE
GAMES

VI

MORE

A good **place to start** with Kurtág's music is short pieces like his *Ligatura message to Frances-Marie op31b*, or the *Games* (*Jatékok*), with their unpredictable spirit and sense of fun, as in 'Les adieux in Janáček's maniere', 'The mad girl with the flaxen hair' or 'Hommage a Nancy Sinatra'.

György Kurtág: Music for String Instruments (ECM records) has a a good selection of his string music which is often surprisingly accessible 'Officium breve in memoriam André Szervanszky' for example

Thomas Adès: Piano (EMI Classics) contains the 'Games' tracks mentioned.

Samples at:

www.amazon.com/exec/obidos/ASIN/B000024R1O/102-0540921-8914545#product-details)

Rudolf Lábán

Pozsony, Hungary (now Bratislava, Slovakia) 1879–1958 Weybridge, England

Dance Educator

'It is impossible to miss the great importance of movement in life' — Rudolph Lábán

Lábán is one of those classic vital figures in British life, the Central European endowed with gifts of talent and high culture that are difficult, apparently, to nourish in the heavy clay of Olde Englande. Earlier he had studied in Paris and had taught in Zurich, Stuttgart and Würzburg, organizing amateur 'movement choirs', then become choreographer at Wagner's Bayreuth Festival. He also created dances for the notorious Berlin Olympiad of 1936, where the current trend for the Olympics and other major sporting events to serve dubious political or commercial ends first manifested itself.

Lábán came to England in 1938, opening a dance studio in Manchester The Art of Movement Studio which is now connected with Goldsmiths College, London. As part of his educational brief he developed a new dance notation system, now known as 'Labanotation'. He can be seen as a parallel figure to Kodály, representing a late burst of the wave of educational and cultural populism that flows through the nineteenth century.

Rudolf Lábán's populism though could be criticized as a little too broad. Although many sources on him rather kindly segue his role working for the Nazis into his subsequent dismissal by Goebbels, it appears that in 1933 he saw the Nazi takeover as an opportunity to advance his dance ideals, and the Nazis admired the 'physicality' of his approach. Coming from an impeccably 'Aryan' Austrian military family, he had no problems on the racial profiling angle, unlike so many other avant-garde cultural figures, including old friends and companions murdered by the Nazis while he was working for them including Erich Mühsam, who he knew at the Utopian colony of Monte Verità alongside Hermann Hesse. He undoubtedly collaborated with the Nazis, so he should be put in that category of artists like Ezra Pound and Céline whose work we may admire but whose political 'innocence' — if that's what it was — should be a warning to all the politically innocent.

MORE

Who's that **chap** with the tiny 'tache you're waltzing with, Rudi?:

Hitler's Dancers. German Modern Dance and the Third Reich Lilian Karina and Marion Kant (2003)

'Modern expressive dance found favor with the regime and especially with the infamous Dr. Joseph Goebbels, the Minister of Propaganda. How modern artists collaborated with Nazism reveals an important aspect of modernism, uncovers the bizarre bureaucracy which controlled culture and tells the histories of great figures who became enthusiastic Nazis and lied about it' (publisher's blurb)

The **official Rudi:**

www.laban.org

More on the 'magic mountain', the Monte Verità art commune:

www.upd.unibe.ch/research/symposien/HA11/monteverita2.html

Imre Lakatos

Debrecen, Hungary 1922–1974 London, England

Ex-prisoner and philosopher of science

Okos disznó mély gyökeret ránt (A clever pig extracts a deep root)

Lakatos was just completing high school as World War Two broke out. By 1944 he had had to change his name from the original Imre Lipschitz and move to Transylvania where he survived the deportations, although his mother and grandmother didn't. As a convinced communist he welcomed the postwar political changes, and even became a party-appointed official at the ministry of education. But by 1950 his critical stance had got him into deep trouble with the Party and he had to spend three years as a political prisoner. He was not released until after Stalin's death in 1953. This period of confinement, as well as his later philosophical work, could be considered as a kind of expiation for his enthusiastic 'clearing out' of non-marxists from important teaching posts when he was at the ministry.

The story becomes a happier one after 1956, when Lakatos escaped to England, starting work in 1960 at the London School of Economics (LSE), a university for the Social Sciences founded by Fabian Socialist activists Beatrice and Sidney Webb with the support of writer Bernard Shaw in 1895.

During the Cold War the LSE became a centre of opposition to intellectual dogmatism, thanks to the work of (Viennese-born) philosopher Karl Popper, Lakatos himself and, later, Prague-born anthropologist and philosopher Ernest Gellner. Lakatos, who had of course had direct experience of the Stalinist Marxist attempt to define truth by *diktat*, eventually devoted himself to the issue of how scientific truth is determined and established. As he said in a famous radio talk, 'Science and pseudoscience', this is more than 'a problem of armchair philosophy'. He cited the cases of the astronomer Copernicus *vs* the Sacred Curia of the Catholic Church, and of the Mendelian biologists *vs* the Central Committee of the Communist Party of the Soviet Union. He asks us not to look not at individual elements of 'falsifiable' data to establish scientificity, positing instead a more sophisticated approach, one that might be called 'holistic' — does the thrust of a 'scientific research programme' predict discoveries yet to be made, in the way that Edmund Halley predicted the path of comets using Isaac Newton's 'programme'.

FOR AND AGAINST METHOD

IMRE LAKATOS
PAUL FEYERABEND

Including Lakatos's Lectures on Scientific Method
and the Lakatos-Feyerabend Correspondence

Communism becomes the butt of his 'how not to do it' examples. He castigates its failure to predict the enrichment of the working class, rather than its impoverishment, or to foresee that revolutions would occur in the underdeveloped countries rather than in the industrialized world, and that conflicts would arise between socialist countries.

The brilliance of Lakatos and other Hungarian émigrés in the fields of philosophy, business and science makes one wonder how much more brilliant Hungary would be today if it had managed to retain all these 'autumn leaves' who were born and bred in the country but were forced by politics or hardship to mature elsewhere.

MORE

That **radio talk** to read:

www.lse.ac.uk/collections/lakatos/scienceAndPseudoscienceTranscript.htm

To **listen to** (with a classic *Mitteleuropaish* accent):

www.lse.ac.uk/collections/lakatos/scienceAndPseudoscience48.mp3

Books:

Lakatos: An Introduction Brendan Larvor (1998)

For and Against Method: Including Lakatos' Lectures on Scientific Method and the Lakatos–Feyerabend Correspondence Imre Lakatos et al (2000)

Hungaro-Brits. The Hungarian Contribution to British Civilisation Mátyás Sárközi (nd, circa 1996)

Estée Lauder
New York, New York, USA 1910–

Queen of cosmetics and weaver of dreams
A shayne ponim kost gelt (A pretty face costs money)

Estée Lauder's story is the Hungamerican dream with all the glitter, flaws and hardness of a diamond. Through amazing acts of self-transformation, energy and what the self-help books call 'focus', Esther Mentzer, daughter of Hungarian Jewish immigrants, went from selling her uncle's face creams door-to-door to heading a huge (but still family-controlled) multinational company selling expensive cosmetics with $4.7 billion sales in 2002. Her first personally engineered product was called 'Youth Dew'® and a current best-seller is 'Futurist Age-Resisting Makeup'®. So what's being sold is clearly the ultimate dream of the narcissist — inextinguishable youth and beauty. But can that be a real product? Anita Roddick of the Body Shop® told us in 2000 that all anti-ageing creams were 'complete pap' and that women worried about their wrinkles would be better off spending the money 'on a good bottle of Pinot noir'.

Estée's (male) children were, naturally, encouraged into the family business, so let's hope they had a natural interest in cosmetics. If not this may be a part of the price that is paid for American Success. Given the relative scarcity of women entrepreneurs at her level of acheivement, Estée Lauder has become an official role model in the USA, celebrated with TV documentaries, praiseful biographies and schoolbooks dedicated to her.

In Jewish Central and Eastern Europe selling was a prime means of family income, as petty trade and market stalls were one of the few areas where Jews (and Jewish women, often the economic mainstay) were allowed to work. Lauder's parents had a department store, so as well as being a 'one-woman marvel' as her biographies have it, she is part of a long European tradition of mercantile ability and experience.

The urbane Estée Lauder still follows her faith and son Ronald is an active Jewish leader and Zionist in the USA, with a plan to irrigate the barren Negev Desert: 'Trains will run from Tel Aviv to Beersheba to Eilat, carrying high-tech wizards to Israel's Silicon Valley and tourists to "a city like Las Vegas",' he recently announced. Whether the Middle East needs a Kosher Vegas is an open question, but somehow it's heartening that the lad doesn't have to dabble with lipstick and face cream anymore, isn't it?

ESTÉE LAUDER

BEAUTY BUSINESS SUCCESS

RACHEL EPSTEIN

MORE

Estée Lauder as **role model**:

Estée Lauder: Beauty Business Success Rachel Epstein (2000)

Another version:

Estée Lauder: beyond the magic: an unauthorized biography Lee Israel (1985)

More **controversy**:

www.longislandpress.com/v01/i30030807/coverstoryb_01.asp

Fans review **the make-up**:

www.makeupalley.com/product/showreview.asp/ItemID=20004/Blush/
Estee_Lauder/Pure_Eden_Blush_Petals/

the **official** site:

www.esteelauder.com/

Ferenc (Franz) Liszt

Doborján, Hungary (now Raiding, Austria) 1811–1886 Bayreuth, Germany

Composer, superstar, superstud

Kemény fából faragták (He was carved of hard wood) — Hungarian saying

Franz Liszt was very rock 'n roll. He toured endlessly and was a virtuoso in a Jimi Hendrix kind of way, regularly playing impossibly, breathlessly fast, so fast that his hands were cast to allow scientific examination of this prodigious creature. Liszt was the first modern musical celebrity, the inventor of the professional piano recital. His showmanship as both performer and composer may have left him today in a somewhat 'Liberace' corner of the classical music canon, popular, enjoyed, but not necessarily respected. Yet he was, like a surprising number of famous Hungarian émigrés, something of an educator or popularizer, with a desire to bring the joys of music to wider audiences.

There was an early start as a pianist and an introduction into exalted circles, as his father worked for Prince Esterházy. He then moved on to a glittering international concert career in London, Switzerland and Paris, breaking it off to deepen his understanding of poetry, philosophy and sociology.

No doubt inspired by all the racy sociology he ran off to Switzerland with the wife of a count. His fame and success had made him feel the equal of any man, a point he had felt he had to prove with a succession of blue-blooded women admirers. Impassioned by his concertistic panache, these regularly fell at his feet. For a decade he was the best-paid and most celebrated pianist in Europe, a wonder of the world for his speed and attack.

Then he settled in Weimar and concentrated on composition, later moving to Rome, where he took minor religious orders as an Abbé. He had enjoyed great acclaim, but, again like many other prominent Hungarians, he was tormented by a search for meaning. Rome, pinnacle of a mighty faith, became the final destination of yet another soul in doubt.

Liszt's music is the true soundtrack for the inner nineteenth century, full of headlong rushes and swooning romantic swells, always searching for excitement and discordant thrills. His famous '*Un sospiro*' for example, is dreamy but unbridled at the same time. Like a lot of nineteenth-century romantic music, it can seem somewhat hysterical today. This may be because we have much more music to listen to now, from the stripped-down of Eric Satie to the lush of Richard Clayderman, whereas Liszt had to use greater firepower to engage with a public who were less musically sophisticated.

MORE

Liszt's Transcendental Studies are considered to be amongst the **most difficult** piano music ever composed

The *Liebestraume* no 3 s.541 for pure inoffensive **charm**

Don't miss: 'Mephisto Walz' and 'St. Francis Preaching to the Birds'

A **masterpiece**: the B Minor Sonata

An interesting **defence** and **appreciation** of Liszt's wider contribution: www.d-vista.com/OTHER/franzliszt2.html

Bela Lugosi (Béla Ferenc Dezső Blaskó)

Lugos, Hungary (now Lugoj, Romania) 1882–1956 Los Angeles, California, USA

Played Jesus Christ and Dracula

Tartozott az ördögnek egy úttal (He owed the devil a journey) — Hungarian saying

Lugosi started his working life as boy miner so knew a thing or two about horror. Breaking into theatre via the operetta chorus and at that point presumably more fresh-faced than in the lugubrious mature version, he played Jesus Christ in a passion play in 1909 and again in 1916. Just as he was scaling the heights of the Budapest theatre World War One broke out. Caught up in the revolutionary fervour of the city in 1919 he cooperated with the short-lived communist regime. With its fall he fled to Germany and then the USA.

Lugosi is well known as the original and fabulous cinematic Dracula ('I never drink wine', 'Children of the night, what music they make') and if his roles at the Budapest national theatre marked the high-point of a Hungarian career his high point in Hollywood was that role in the 1931 film directed by another great Hollywood figure, Tod Browning — who, incidentally, made perhaps the most unusual and humane film in its history, the long-forbidden *Freaks* (1932). Some other noted roles followed in; *Murders in the Rue Morgue* (1932), *White Zombie* (1932), *Island of Lost Souls* (1933), and *Mark of the Vampire* (1935) until his triumph as the crazed Ygor in *Son of Frankenstein* (1939).

Afterwards, sad to relate, there was a long slide downwards through costly divorces, B-movies, drug addiction and unemployment which was only 'halted' by his being adopted by another rather unique director, Edward D. Wood Jr, who directed him in *Glen or Glenda* (1953), an awesomely bad 'mockumentary' on transvestism, starring Wood himself in a skirt, and then a final appearance in the famous 'world's worst film', *Plan 9 from Outer Space.* This was created, appropriately enough for a *revenant,* after Lugosi's death in 1956 using footage shot for another of Wood's projects.

Lugosi died shortly after being hospitalized for his morphine addiction, a genuine horror ending to his story.

MORE
'The Chamber of Doctor Werdegast', an excellent Lugosi **site**:
www.geocities.com/Hollywood/Set/6240/bio.html
Documentary on Lugosi and Dracula:
www.dvdreview.com/quickpeek/collect/745.shtml
The **1931 Dracula** masterpiece on DVD:
www.rottentomatoes.com/m/Dracula-1006234/dvd.php

Sándor Márai

Kassa, Hungary (now Košice, Slovakia) 1900–1989 San Diego, California, USA

The strange case of a literary revenant

Isten malmai lassan őrölnek, de biztosan (The mills of God grind slowly, but surely)

The fate of Sándor Márai, a great writer chased away from his country by an intolerant regime, who spent forty years in increasingly lonely exile on another continent, might be a metaphor for Hungary's own fate. Many years after it was written, his work, in particular that masterpiece of friendship, memory and ageing, his novel *Embers*, is becoming recognized as a humane and profound contribution to Europe's serious literature.

The Hungarian literary tradition in which Márai wrote, was essentially created in the nineteenth century but resounds with many ancient folkloric elements and explores Hungary's peculiar condition as an old-new land, populated by a relatively recently arrived ethnic group (the Magyars). A land with a late-lingering feudalism — but also a place where radical political experiments of liberal, communist and fascist stamp have been tried — it continually reminds us, like some great forest, of the ancient continuities of landscape and way of life that surround modernity. The (now) international bestselling *Embers* is itself a meditation on the problematic survival of older codes of loyalty, both to symbols and between coevals, masters and servants, lovers, husbands and wives.

The exile Márai called the Hungarian language his 'only homeland'. He lived immersed in it to the end, but also apart from it, refusing to return home until free elections had taken place and all Soviet troops had left. He committed suicide before this happened, but now in the same way that Márai's work is rejoining our European community, so is Hungary. Judging by its writers' literary achievements, we will be greatly enriched.

MORE

Translations:

Embers (2002) tr. from German by C.B.Janeway

Memoir of Hungary 1944-48 tr., & notes Albert Tezla (1996)

Conversations in Bolzano translated by G.Szirtes will be published by Viking in 2004 or 2005

Hungarian literature in English translation see: babelguides.com

Forthcoming **film** of *Embers* directed by Milos Forman:

www.thezreview.co.uk/comingsoon/e/embers.htm

Margaret of Scotland

Mecseknádas, Hungary 1045–1093 Edinburgh, Scotland

High-flying Hungarian émigré: Queen and Saint (canonized 1250)

Minden út Rómába vezet (All roads lead to Rome)

Margaret's life shows that there is no upper limit for a high-flying Hungarian, especially if she doesn't mind Pictish behaviour and a coolish climate, y'ken. It helps if you have a suitable family background: her dad was heir to the throne of England.

In those days England was more like twentieth-century Hungary or twenty-first century Iraq, experiencing régime change and foreign occupations. Between the Danes and the Normans (1066 and all that), Margaret's family's chance to rule in England fell by the wayside, so they attempted to flee back to Hungary. But their ship, blown off course, eventually arrived in Scotland, where a certain Macbeth had been recently deposed and King Malcolm ruled. The twenty-four-year-old Margaret, according to hagiography at least, wished to become a nun, but was dissuaded by Malcolm who married her instead. Lanfranc, the Benedictine who later became Archbishop of Canterbury, advised her on the reform of the Church in Scotland. While Margaret was familiar with Latin, her husband, known as Ceann mor, or Big Head was an illiterate warrior-king whose moodiness was counterbalanced by her pious and calming influence.

Scotland had been separated from the rest of Europe by the Anglo-Saxons, and later by the Danish invasions of England. During these periods the Scottish and Irish churches had developed their own non-standard practices, including the use of Gaelic rather than Latin in the liturgy. Margaret made it her mission, with the help of Norman advisers, to stamp out all these irregularities, so perhaps she should be seen as an early proponent of the European project in its least attractive standardizing mode. Unlike much of the European periphery Scotland had not been colonized by the Normans. Through their religious and cultural influence though they made Scotland much closer to England and Europe than geographical isolation and the largely Celtic heritage might otherwise have predicted.

Margaret bore eight children and is the only female saint to have experienced motherhood.

MORE

Prayer to Saint Margaret at:

justus.anglican.org/resources/bio/284.html

Historical background:

www.electricscotland.com/history/scotland/chap2.htm

Going back to **Celtic Christianity** at:

www.gaelicweb.com/irishampost/year2002/02february/featured/
featured01.html

George Mikes
Siklós, Hungary 1912–1987 London, England

Piss-taker or patriot?

'In all the miseries which plague mankind there is hardly anything better than such radiant humour as is given to you'.— Albert Einstein (Letter to Mikes after reading *How To Be An Alien*)

George Mikes, grateful to escape the wartime inferno of his homeland and settle in Britain spent the rest of his life taking the mickey out of his hosts, the English ('Continental people have sex lives; the English have hot-water bottles'), making a fortune with his *How To Be An Alien* (1946) and then continued the assault in further books like *Italy for Beginners* (1956), taking the piss out of the rest of Europe, the Americans, the Japanese etc.

Taking the piss out of allied nations would clearly have been much trickier if Mikes had stayed on in the Eastern and Central Europe of the Warsaw Pact. A famous joke has Churchill telling Stalin at Yalta in 1945: 'D'you know I collect the jokes people make about me! Stalin replies: 'Really! And I collect the people who make jokes about me.'

Why did the gentle mockery of *How To Be An Alien* go down so well? The aftermath of World War Two was the great pricking of the imperial British bubble. The country was broke from the burden of war debts. 'Unimaginably', British troops had been defeated by an Asian army in the Far East (the Fall of Singapore) and the Indian 'Jewel in the Crown' was being reclaimed by the rightful owners. All that was left was vainglory, the pompous coronation of Elizabeth II, the ascent of Everest by a sub-Briton (actually a New Zealander) with Sherpa leg-up, and then a good deal of earnest Labour social engineering (the NHS, town planning and so on). The time was ripe for George Mikes, the sardonic, sophisticated son of another deceased empire, like a Greek philosopher in Ancient Rome or a Cervantes in tottering post-glorious Spain, to orchestrate the laughter at the stiff upper lip, awkwardness and civilized barbarity of imperial Britishry.

Is America's George Mikes growing up today somewhere in Tallinn, Vientiane or Khartoum?

MORE

Funny books by Mikes:

How To Be An Alien (1946)

How to be Seventy (1982)

Not so funny:

A study in infamy: the operations of the Hungarian Secret Police (AVO) based on secret documents issued by the Hungarian Ministry of the Interior (1959)

Quotes:

www.amusingquotes.com/h/m/George_Mikes_1.htm

András Pető
Szombathely, Hungary 1893–1967 Budapest, Hungary
Educator
'Give a fish to a hungry man and you will save him from starvation today. Teach him to fish. He and his family will prosper and be happy for a lifetime.' — the motto of Dr. András Pető

Isn't 'educator' one of the proudest titles a man or woman could hold? Educators find a way to help others to knowledge, independence, culture. András Pető made amazing progress in tackling the learning difficulties experienced by handicapped or differently-abled children, a very special group who interact with the rest of us in a way that tests our humanity. A test demonstrated by the attitude of perhaps the least human bunch ever seen on our planet, the Nazis, who saw them as fit only to be exterminated. Pető and his collaborators in Hungary show the other, glorious extreme, by finding the way to connect better with people who are of us but in some way different.

It is appropriate that András Pető started his first educational institute in a basement in war-ravaged Budapest in the same year (1945) that saw the defeat of those who Wilhelm Reich called 'the little men', who refuse the humanity of people they see as different.

Pető's system — pioneered in Hungary and still based there — assumes that specialised intensive education can overcome the effects of injury to the central nervous system, for instance the kind that prevents people from sitting up. Pető-trained educators or 'conductors' fine-tune the teaching method to adapt it for the individual as well as for children working in groups.

Like many great innovators Pető found his way intuitively and through experience. He discovered that useful neural pathways can be created from doing and learning and are not simply biological givens as previously assumed. Similarly, recent studies show that the very old retain much better memory function if constantly intellectually challenged and prompted.

Pető's work reveals in a moving way the potential of learning through solidarity and of faith in human capacity, he rejected the idea that motor dysfunction was biological and irreversible and always asserted there were 'no hopeless cases.'

MORE

Today:

The Pető Institute in Budapest is still flourishing and is at the heart of a world network of similar institutes for 'conductive education'. It is also the main centre for learning the special skills of teaching Pető's method.

www.petoinstitute.org/english/pastpresent/index.html

Karl Polányi

Vienna, Austria 1886–1964 Pickering, Ontario, Canada

Social scientist

Nem mind arany, ami fénylik (All that glisters is not gold)

With the ending of the Cold War it could be said that the old Right/ Left divide makes less and less sense. The collapse of the command economy model (those famous Ukrainian sock factories that only made left feet, as long as quotas were kept up) means that the 'debate' is reduced to applause for 'the free market'. Yet this isn't a cure-all for poorer countries which don't possess the infrastructure (or is it the political muscle?) to get favourable trading conditions.

Hence a lot of rather woolly debate about 'globalization'. Addressing the problems of quality of life *vs* rate of profit, the mercurial and polymathic journalist, educator, economic historian and anthropologist Karl Polányi took a more profound and historical approach as early as 1944, in works like *The Great Transformation*. Unlike most other writing dealing with economic history this looked at the Ancient World, China and Africa in order to situate the 'market' and the market process in a wider social and cultural context. Using this broader view Polányi lamented the destruction of the traditional cultural practices that provided livelihoods, the management of the land and various socially useful skills, by what he saw as the capture of political authority — of the state power essentially — by the trading elite to make it serve the market mechanism. Quite possibly Polányi's books and the debate he started now have an essential role in helping us to make *social* decisions about the economy. His vision also seems to tie in with Ivan Illich's work on the 'de-skilling' of society by state-regulated professions, and with the ecological critics of 'unlimited growth'.

It's no coincidence that such fruitful ideas should have come from a Hungarian who, typically for his harried generation with their disrupted lives and careers, also lived and studied in Austria, England, Canada and the USA. He was a man who spanned disciplines, professions, East and West, ancient and modern history, as well as what is now called the South and North...

With great prescience he wrote in 1958 'The subordination of science and technology, as well as economic organisation, to our will to human progress and to the fulfilment of personality, has become a requirement of survival.' Speaking as an inhabitant of the Land of the Mad Cow and as a fan of New York, just one of many cities threatened by global warming, the question of 'survival' he posed for us then still seems as open today.

MORE

Major works of Karl Polányi:

The Great Transformation (1944)

Trade and Markets in Early Empires, with K. Conrad, K. Arensburg and H.W. Pearson (1957)

Dahomey and the Slave Trade with A. Rotstein (1966)

Primitive, Archaic and Modern Economics: Essays of Karl Polányi (1968)

The Livelihood of Man with H.W. Pearson (1977)

Resources on Karl Polányi:

Karl Polányi Institute for Political Economy at Concordia University

cepa.newschool.edu/het/profiles/polanyi.htm

Giorgio Pressburger

Budapest, Hungary 1937–

Spinner of worlds and languages, true son of *Mitteleuropa*

Tutto è bene quello che finisce bene (All's well that ends well)

A Hungarian writing in Italian and translated into English (and French, German, Spanish etc. etc.) revealed to the world the intense life of Jewish Budapest before the Holocaust. In an extraordinary trio of books (*Homage to the Eighth District, The Law of White Spaces* and *The Green Elephant*), the first two written with his twin Nicola, Giorgio Pressburger recreated in a detached, picaresque style quite foreign to Italian traditions the city he'd known as a child, before departing for Turin in 1956.

The Eighth District of Budapest was populated by the poorer sort of Jews. From their ranks pop up in these books indefatigble market women, the local icy beauty and heartbreaker Ilona Weiss, *luftmentshn* ('air-men') like Franja, who make a living out of thin air and, reaching back into a fecund tradition of ironic Jewish storytelling (Rabbi Nachman, Sholem Aleichem, I.L. Peretz) the beatific starveling scholar Nathan who climbs up the mystic tree of the Zohar* itself. The theme of mystical redemption in a harsh world is continued in the charming *Green Elephant,* which explores, largely from a child's point of view, the comforting idea of the Messiah for an exiled and oppressed people.

After working in the theatre and broadcasting Giorgio Pressburger settled in Trieste. So, unlike many familiar names from the 1956 exile generation, he has managed to remain in *Mitteleuropa* — the 'Central Europe' that forms the approximate area of the old Austro-Hungarian Empire, an intellectually fertile, if conflictual, community of many peoples. Remaining there has enabled him to run a yearly cultural festival called *Mittelfest.* Held in Friuli, (north-eastern Italy) with enormous success it brings together a wide variety of art and artists from that 'culture zone'.

Finally — in a heartening sign that not every Central European destiny must for ever be entirely fractured, Giorgio Pressburger was appointed to head the *Istituto Italiano di Cultura*, the cultural arm of the Italian government abroad, in Budapest in 1998.

*The Zohar is a Jewish mystical text upon which much of kabbalistic magic and spirituality is based

Giorgio e Nicola Pressburger

L'elefante verde

EINAUDI TASCABILI

MORE

Giorgio Pressburger **in Hungary:**

www.ofi.hu/index.ofi?mfa_id=164&hir_id=2215

Reviews of the Pressburger translations above in the *Babel Guide to Italian Fiction* (1998) and at babelguides.com

Mittelfest site:

www.regione.fvg.it/mittelfest/

Italian Cultural Institute Budapest (site in Hungarian and Italian):

www.datanet.hu/iic/

Joseph Pulitzer

Makó, Hungary 1847–1911, Charleston, South Carolina, USA

Prototypical Press Baron

A nagy hal megeszi a kis halat (The big fish eats the little fish)

Pulitzer was active in the deepest, darkest parts of the nineteenth century, beginning his newspaper career in that obscure fringe of mass journalism the foreign-language daily (the *Westliche Post* of Saint Louis Missouri which catered for German immigrants). Prototypical, maybe, but also fairly typical, he possessed the basic business *nous* of buying and selling — he bought the *Post*, then sold it back to the original owner, making a $30,000 profit. His later career buying up newspapers and dominating press markets demonstrates the facility of ownership concentration in the new technologies of the time.

Even in such a vast country as the USA, the power of money, good business sense and the manipulation of markets and capital can rapidly create a situation in which only a few sources of information remain. In Britain for example, quite apart from the small number of national media centres such as Rupert Murdoch's News International, a huge number of local titles are now owned by a large US corporation, Gannet. To cite an example, in one prosperous small British city the two local weeklies, the daily, the local FM station and the two freesheets all belong to the same company. The independent 'competition' is a huge government-owned corporation, the BBC, with its local radio and its news website.

The trail Pulitzer blazed was to work on the visual technology of selling the news, refining the use of headlines, pictures and page layout. He multiplied the sales of his flagship paper the *New York World* an astounding tenfold in five years. He worked his advertisers, reducing the newstand price to increase circulation and attract the big spending department stores. This enriched him and professionalized, in a certain way, the press. It also reduced the diversity of newspaper production. Today some of the world's largest and richest cities (including Los Angeles and London) have only one local daily.

The irony is that as press barons and corporations have come and gone the Pulitzer name remains as the label both on an award and on a famous school for quality independent journalism — surely the one thing that the 'Pulitzerist' monopolization of the media is most liable to destroy.

MORE

Excellent **background article** on Joseph Pulitzer:

www.onlineconcepts.com/pulitzer/frontpg.htm

Book:

Joseph Pulitzer and the New York World George Juergens (1966).

Pulitzer awards site:

www.pulitzer.org

The Columbia Graduate **School of Journalism**

www.jrn.columbia.edu

History of the **Pulitzer** Journalism School:

Pulitzer's School Columbia University's School of Journalism, 1903-2003
James Boylan (2003)

Ferenc Puskás

Budapest, Hungary 1927–

Famous fat footballer

'We were not fairly beaten, my lord. No Englishman is ever fairly beaten.' — George Bernard Shaw

The usual tradition in English writing about English history is not to dwell too much on defeats. Remember Yorktown 1781? The Ashanti Wars? No, I didn't think you would. Alternatively, we turn a defeat into a victory gracefully deferred (Dunkirk). However in this case that's really hard to do. They beat us fair and square. So let's break with tradition and admit this terrible and unanticipated defeat. In 1953, for the first time ever, a foreign team beat England at home, in Wembley stadium. It was an extraordinary football squad from Hungary, known as the 'Golden Team', who won all their international matches four years running. It was led by an even more extraordinary individual, a squat, overweight chap called Ferenc Puskás who scored eighty-three goals in eighty-four internationals — more even than Pelé — only ever using his left foot (the right foot 'is just for standing on', he quipped) and never giving a header.

On the day of disaster in 1953, Puskas was appraised thus by an England player: 'Look at that little fat chap. We'll murder this lot.' After all England had invented and taught the world this game, recently crowned a spanking new monarch, conquered Everest and, on the cultural front, Agatha Christie's *The Mousetrap* had already been wowing audiences for six months — from such heights the fall was great: England beaten 6-3 by the happy Hungarians.

Puskás, like a lot of his nifty compatriots, fled to Vienna in 1956, having tired of being paraded as a socialist success story (maybe the communists were a bit short of them). He eventually signed up with Real Madrid and invested his match fees in a sausage factory.

Puskás and some of his team mates had amazing natural talents but the team was also well drilled and had a good tactical approach. The English lacked preparation and tactics, proceeding in the ninety-year-old tradition of amateur gymnastics. They were unprepared for an age in which sport was played for Cold War brownie points, and was a significant part of communist foreign policy which notoriously saw East German coaches feeding their young protégés with damaging steroid concoctions.

A great Hungarian victory but maybe a defeat for the ideal of sport as fellowship and fun. There now, I've turned a foreign victory into a moral defeat. God Save the Queen!

PUSKAS
on Puskas

The Life and Times of
a Footballing Legend

edited by
ROGAN TAYLOR AND KLARA JAMRICH

MORE

Ferenc Puskás and inumerable other **'Soccer Saints'**:

www.soccersaints.com/leg44.htm

Also **here**:

www.thehistoryof.co.uk/People/Footballers/Ferenc_Puskas.html

Buy the **book**

Puskas on Puskas: The Life & Times of a Footballing Legend (1997)

Árpád Pusztai

Budapest, Hungary 1930–

GM whistleblower and scientific (anti?)-hero

Meg állja a sarat (He stands the test) — Hungarian saying

After two centuries of madcap scientific advance — mustard gas, expanded polystyrene and leaf blowers spring to mind — some folk are getting a queasy feeling. One of the queasiest is to worry about what exactly is happening to our food nowadays. Don't let them f**k with your food! So said (as it were) the brave Hungarochamp Árpád Pusztai, a biotechnologist courageous enough to stick his nose over the parapet in a world where research science is largely funded by 'hungry' corporations and almost equally short-sighted and ethically challenged government ministries.

Originally a firm believer in the benefits of GM technology, Pusztai was paid to head up a large government research project into its safety. When he found that in the case he studied (genetically modified potatoes), there was an alarming unpredictability in the eventual outcome, that the genome could appear in different places and generate possibly worrying effects in this 'safe, stable' technology there was panic from quarters firm in their appreciation of these techniques including the British Government and the bio-corporations that deal in modified seeds.

Clumsy moves were made to silence Pusztai, who had come to England in 1956 because it smelt to him of liberty and freedom of speech.

The debate goes on, with Europeans increasingly wary of the so-called 'Frankenstein foods', the long-term benefits of which are much easier to see if you are a shareholder in a company that has invested in this particular technology. Hunger, certainly one of the world's most serious issues, is held to be a justification for GM. But previous hi-tech fixes like 'the green revolution' have failed, because hunger has many causes above and beyond crop yields per hectare — as was understood by the Ancient Egyptians, Mayans and Romans who maintained huge granaries against bad years. These civilizations also had transport and distribution systems that are lacking in many of today's hungry areas of the world.

MORE

The **basic story** on Puzstai and GM:
www.global-reality.com/biotech/articles/news106.htm
More at:
www.global-reality.com/biotech/othernews.asp
A more sanguine view of GM at:
groups.yahoo.com/group/plantbiotechnology/message/123
You eats your potatoes and takes your pick (**Puzstai speaks**):
www.actionbioscience.org/biotech/pusztai.html

Miklós Radnóti

Budapest, Hungary 1909–1944 Abda, Hungary

Stooge or Saint?

'Slowly the eye relinquishes the bounds of our captivity' — Radnóti in *Forced March*

Scratch a Hungarian and you often find a Hungarian Jew underneath. How this double-identity works could be the subject of an entire book. Miklós Radnóti's life was a tragic coda on that theme. A Jewish poet who dedicated himself to the Hungarian lyric, converted to the Catholic religion with its long ambivalence toward the Jewish people and finally perished on a forced march ('The squad stands about in knots, stinking, mad/ Death, hideous, is blowing overhead.')* organized by the Hungarian fascists, the Arrow Cross.

The Jewish contribution to Hungary's cultural, economic and political life has been considerable. But it's a story not unlike the German-Jewish one, often achieved at the cost of assimilation. Hungarians of Jewish descent gave unstintingly to the richness of the Hungarian nation. Their reward? From a high point during the later years of the Austro-Hungarian empire, when Jewish families, businessmen, writers and even military men flourished, the post-World War One government of Admiral Horthy passed a succession of cruelly depreciative anti-Semitic laws such as the *numerus clausus*, that kept Radnóti himself out of Budapest University (only 6 per cent of the student body could be Jewish).

Yet Radnóti was determined to enjoy and celebrate what he sensed would be a prematurely doomed existence, leaving us the verbal beauty of a poet in love: '…here, through a sprinkle of pearly and delicate sunrays/ shimmers the infinite blue of your eyes…'**

Extraordinarily the poet worked in both classical and modernist verse forms, as well as being a noted translator. Publishing acclaimed books of poetry throughout the 1930s he was murdered in his prime but his work is now a growing influence on younger writers. George Szirtes, who has the advantage of knowing his work in the original, considers that 'Radnóti, together with Paul Celan, is…the greatest poet of World War Two'.

His last great poetry, collected in *Forced March*, was recovered from a bloodstained notebook found on his body, disinterred from a mass grave. Shortly before his death he had written: '…How strange that I'm alive. A bland efficient death searches this age,/ and they turn white on whom it lays its hand'*** A self-penned epitaph for Radnóti and for a whole generation of intellectuals, poets, artists, musicians slaughtered by fascism from one end of the continent in Spain to the battlefields and ghettos of Russia at the other.

*From 'Razglednicas' in *Foamy Sky. The Major Poems of Miklós Radnóti*, (1992), p118

** From 'Love Poem' p45 *ibid.*

*** from *Foamy Sky* p50 *ibid.*

MORE

The poetry

Forced March tr.Clive Wilmer and George Gömöri (2003)
(A **new edition** of this book will be launched 01/12/2003 at the New End Theatre, Hampstead): www.enitharmon.co.uk

Foamy Sky, The Major Poems of Miklós Radnóti selected and translated by Z.Ozváth & F.Turner (1992)

Camp notebooks (Parallel English and Hungarian text) tr. Francis R. Jones introduced by George Szirtes (2000)

The Seventh Eclogue:

benturner.com/genesis/poem_foamy.html

The **man** and **his work**

In the Footsteps of Orpheus: The Life and Times of Miklós Radnóti by Zsuzsanna Ozsvath (2001)

The Poetry of Miklós Radnóti: A Comparative Study Emery Edward George (1986)

The Life and Poetry of Miklós Radnóti Essays Edited by George Gomori and Clive Wilmer (1999)

An **online resource on Hungarian poetry in Translation**

pigeon.cch.kcl.ac.uk/mpt/Tr.Hung1.html

Radnóti High School Szeged, Hungary

www.radnoti-szeged.sulinet.hu/torta/tort30.htm

A **film** *Forced March* directed by Rick King in 1989 tells in part the Radnóti story

www.tvguide.com/movies/database/showmovie.asp?MI=34113

Géza Róheim

Budapest, Hungary 1891–1953, New York, New York, USA

Anthropologist and psychoanalyst

'Sometimes a cigar is just a cigar' — Sigmund Freud

No doubt because Austria-Hungary was famously run on secretive and conspiratorial lines, in an effort to preserve it in the face of rising nationalism from every quarter — Italians in Trieste, Czechs in Bohemia, Poles in Galicia and so forth — it seems to have engendered a tribe of explorers who shone a light into every crevice of society (philosophers, journalists), nature (chemists, physicists) and humanity itself (doctors, psychologists). Vienna was, of course, the epicentre of Freud and psychoanalysis, a brave attempt — if variously in and out of fashion — to probe the darkest corners of the psyche.

One of many Hungarian pioneers associated with psychoanalysis was Géza Róheim, originally not a couch-curer but an anthropologist. Perhaps his in-depth investigating started at the age of twelve when his father opened an account for him at Budapest's leading bookshop. One aspect of the nationalism of the empire's peoples — including that of the Hungarians — was a burgeoning interest in folklore. This is where Róheim's anthropology began. Very rapidly afterwards came an interest in psychoanalysis. Then the most eminent anthropologist of the time, Bronislaw Malinowski, launched an attack on the universality of Freud's crucial theory of the Oedipus complex, denying its existence in the Pacific Ocean societies he had studied. This led to Freud commissioning Róheim (who in the meantime had lost his university teaching position in Hungary for political reasons) to set out with his wife Ilonka on an extraordinary fieldwork tour. They crossed Arabia, Australia, the Pacific and North America (where Róheim studied Amerindians), financed by Freud's sponsor the Princess Bonaparte, a descendant of Napoleon. Fortunately Róheim managed to prove that Oedipus had indeed sailed the Pacific seas.

Possibly of more interest is that in a second career as a psychoanalytical psychiatrist in an American mental hospital, Róheim worked on a theory that the fertile symbolism adopted by some schizophrenics may illustrate the original working of the human mind in the creation of the symbolic realm. This suggests that therefore all culture and language, although undoubtedly useful, is at the same time merely a 'fevered invention', play, mad, mutable magic.

Animism, Magic and the Divine King
(1930)

Geza Roheim

MORE

Books:

Nach dem Tode des Urvaters (Toward the Death of the Primal Fathers) (1923)
Australian Totemism (1925)
Animism, Magic, and the Divine King (1930).
The Origin and Function of Culture (1943).
Psychoanalysis and Anthropology (1950)
The Gates of the Dream (1952)
Magic and Schizophrenia (1955).
Substantial **site** on Róheim and '*Ethnopsychologie*':
perso.wanadoo.fr/geza.roheim/html/ethnopsy.htm
Forgotten your French? Try;
orpheus.ucsd.edu/speccoll/testing/html/mss0046d.html

Egon Ronay

Pozsony, Hungary (now Bratislava, Slovakia) 1915–

Journalist and preventative medicine pioneer

Amit főztél, edd is meg (What you have cooked you should eat yourself)

Those who know the Hungarian way of eating — rich, abundant and generous — are not surprised that it was a Hungarian émigré, Egon Ronay, descended from a long line of Budapest and countryside restaurateurs and hotel proprietors who, in 1957 started a protracted campaign to improve the standards of restaurant cooking and service in Britain. After years of publishing the famous Egon Ronay Restaurant Guides he shifted his attention to those everyday but often lamentable eating spaces: airports and motorway service stations. His secret weapon was, as before, his team of anonymous inspectors who subject themselves to the same culinary experience as Joe Punter and his Missus. He also bravely investigated the Macdonald's® and Burger King® hamburger chains. There he was forced to report that the burgers, if not necessarily some of the salads and accoutrements, were 'inedible'.

Food quality is essentially a matter of tradition, of practices of raising, growing, preparing and using edibles that develop a tasty and practical culinary 'product' over the centuries. That is how regional and national cuisines are built up. There are no short cuts. All the modern tricks just don't work. Flying in stale Mexican peppers and larding them on to a defrosted pizza base doesn't create anything beyond bare nutrition. Ronay knew this in his bones. In an interview he revealed that at all the meetings he attended about his family restaurants back in Hungary, profit margins were never mentioned — his father had become wealthy in the business because the quality of food offered was high not because he set out to 'maximize inputs'.

So we salute Egon Ronay, friend to everyone who eats, as 'the man who prevented a thousand stomach ulcers'. Meanwhile 80 per cent of British homes have a microwave... Ready-made omelette in a packet, anyone?

MORE

Ronay eats in **burger hell:**

www.ananova.com/news/story/sm_702102.html

Ronay eats **on Concorde:**

www.xent.com/FoRK-archive/winter96/0014.html

Memories are made of this:

The Unforgettable Dishes of My Life Egon Ronay (1989)

Ernő Rubik

Budapest, Hungary 1944–

Promoter of dull but harmless 'fun'

A határ a csillagos ég (The sky's the limit)

Surely yet another Hungarian ahead of his time, prefiguring the GameBoy® and suchlike, although we might say that Ernő Rubik's eponymous masterpiece was itself prefigured by activities like getting the knots out of a piece of string, the nails out of a worthwhile bit of pre-owned board or even the sand out of the sandwiches (at the beach) and similar lengthy but essentially empty routines.

Despite the fact that one hundred million cubes have been sold, and that a die-hard Rubiker's club exists in Holland to this day, the famous cube has indeed been replaced by things like the GameBoy® — which is hugely more sophisticated and fun. But still, in the cube's favour, no batteries to buy, right?

Rubik studied as an architect and developed the cube in 1974 while working as a lecturer at the Academy of Applied Arts and Crafts in Budapest from a desire to demonstrate design projects in three dimensions. The invention was to make him the richest man in Hungary. Outside the design studio the main purpose of these devices which one could call *passatiempos* in Spanish or 'time-wasters' in English, is to entertain those too intellectually challenged to open a newspaper or God-in-Heaven-forbid a *book*, while stuck on the tube or bus. On overground transport the necessity for entertaining the illiterate has passed to the mobile phone ('Hello Mum I'm on the train'). This has the advantage for fellow travellers of making much more noise (and therefore entertainment) than the mere pinging of a GameBoy®, whereas a well-greased Rubik, like an assassin's knife, is silent.

Of interest today (possibly) is the existence of a huge virtual Rubikland on the Internet. This offers puzzle solutions, excerpts from record-breaking cube solutions (presently we're looking at 16.3 seconds in the 2003 World Championship) and explorations of the mathematics behind the cube, as well as how to fix a broken or chipped one.

Some psychiatrists claim that autism and the milder aspergism are vastly on the increase, and ten minutes in the dry canyons of Virtual Rubikaia will persuade you of this, unless they are *all* nine-year-old boys behind these sites.

Let's hope so. And if not at least they won't chat for long on their mobiles. They're not really touchy-feely, walky-talky types.

MORE

Dispatches from the Republic of Rubikaia:

The world **record!**

www.recordholders.org/en/list/rubik.html

Read all about it in **Interlingua** ('Nostre Rekord-Klub SAXONIA ha essite fundate in 1988. Il ha un regula stricte que tote membro debe esser un battitor de record mundial')

www.recordholders.org/ia/index.html

The **official** site

rubiks.com

Claude-Michel Schoenberg

Vannes, France 1944–

Composer

Akinek a szekerén ülsz, annak a nótáját fújjad (Sing the song of the man whose cart you sit on)

Schoenberg, working with his partner, Tunisian Alain Boubil, composed the music for the tremendously successful *Les Misérables*. He had previously produced in 1973, on the model of *Hair* and *Jesus Christ Superstar,* a best-selling concept work on 1789 and all that, thereby turning the French Revolution, beacon for oppressed humanity for two hundred years and inspiration of all subsequent revolutions, into a long-playing record.

Having 'done' the French Revolution he and Boubil turned their attention to another iconic part of French cultural history, the famous novel by Victor Hugo, *Les Misérables*. Later, with their *Miss Saigon*, the same trick: the most noted and tragic war of the late twentieth century turned into, yes, a musical.

'I'm a Hungarian Jew who happens to have been born in France', Schoenberg told us on the BBC radio interview programme 'Desert Island Discs'. When asked which luxury he would take with him to the castaway's island him he said: 'Kosher pálinka!'* Isn't there an endearingly grateful second-generation immigrant element about his rather old-fashioned celebration of the icons of the new *patrie*? Like the folk who founded Hollywood and have succeeded in drowning the world's cinema, with all its diverse narrative, poetic and national elements, in globalised treacle (or shmalts* which is less sticky and more sickly).

Popular success but not critical success, this too is reminiscent of Hollywood, and Schoenberg and Boubil have been 'exiled' from France to the Anglo-Saxon cultural camp where their work, despite its French extraction, is vastly more popular and profitable. The entertainment industry always prefers pop pap to 'arty crap' — when it's a question of bums on seats, a punter with a head and a critical brain is not really required. Is this being unfair to M. Schoenberg's *oeuvre*? Both the lyrics and music have been described as 'unmemorable', we don't have musical facilities on this page so judge from the lyrics (by Herbert Kretzmer); 'Take my hand and lead me to salvation/ Take my love/ for love is everlasting/ And remember the truth that once was spoken/ To love another person/ is to see the face of God.' From the section called 'The Death' in *Les Misérables*, and this is truly deathless stuff.

Pálinka. A fruit brandy made in Hungary

**shmalts* or *Schmalz* is literally rendered chicken fat, soft, white and gooey

V.Hugo

MORE

About **pálinka:**

www.talkingcities.co.uk/budapest_pages/food_drink_wine.htm

Drink **Kosher Szilva Pálinka** at the Old Europeans Resaturant 106 High Road, London N2:

www.oldeuropeans.com/dessert.htm

Buy the **song sheets** for *Les Misérables*, why not?

www.sheetmusicplus.com/a/
phrase.html?id=68820&phrase=Les%20Miserables

George Soros
Budapest, Hungary 1930–
Financier and philanthropist
A pénznek nincs szaga (Money has no smell)

It would be splendid if those two labels *financier* and *philanthropist* went together more often than they do. But when a very wealthy man or woman does decide to find and to fund a good cause (rather than a third wife/husband, TV station, mansion with gold taps in bathroom etc.) then the benefits can be considerable. This author, for one, discovered the glories of our cultural heritage reading in several of Andrew Carnegie's public library buildings.*

But then again, George Soros proves the old saw: 'there's just no pleasing some folks'. Soros, a Hungarian Jew from Budapest, decided to spend a good part (he had given away $2.8 billion by early 2001) of the fortune he made as the world's most successful currency speculator, bankrolling new institutions in Eastern and Central Europe. His aim was to aid the transition to democracy and rebuild a civic society ruined by years of fascist and communist authoritarianism and arbitrary power. One of these institutions was the Central European University which 'promotes a system of education in which ideas are creatively, critically, and comparatively examined'. Another was *Solidarnosc* in Poland. And latterly he has financed independent TV channels in ex-Yugoslavia. Certain locals sagely concluded that this was all a one-man Zionist plot to lord it over the hallowed mud of the glorious fatherland. Poor old George — his public-spirited generosity strained the limits of the anti-Semitic mind. It was all clearly a *youknowhoish* plot to take over Central Europe ('again'?).

Endearingly Soros, much inspired by Karl Popper, the LSE philosopher-king who laboured to debunk the facile systemization of 'Marxist methodology', tried to build a career outside the world of stocks, shares and the tumble of financial dice by becoming an intellectual-with-an-accent. Here is the endearing bit — he realized he simply wasn't up to it. In his book *Soros on Soros* he recounts: 'There came a day when I was rereading what I had written the day before, and I couldn't make sense of it.' Now did that ever stop an academic before?

*Andrew Carnegie, Scottish-American millionaire who, by the time of his death in 1919, had given away over $350 million to provide free libraries, church organs, schools and colleges.

MORE

The Central European University:

www.ceu.hu

From the **horse's mouth:**

Soros on Soros George Soros, Byron Wien, Krisztina Koenen (1995)

Alan Deutschman's **excellent article** on Soros

www.salon.com/archives/2001/date03.html

István Szabó

Budapest, Hungary 1938–

Film Director

A sólyom madárnak nem lesz galamb fia (A falcon will not breed a dove)

The Hungarian cinema of the 1970s, like the cinema of Poland and Czechoslovakia, benefited from a certain liberalism of the Communist authorities that allowed films to be made that were interesting enough to be welcomed abroad, providing Westerners with a rare contact with the cultural world behind the Iron Curtain. Filmmakers like Jancso were widely respected outside Hungary. More recently István Szabó has managed to create an auteurish and thematic opus in his films *Redl, Mephisto, Sonnenschein* and *Taking Sides*. While they are situated in the particular conditions and locales of central Europe (they are set in Bohemia, Berlin and Budapest) they also raise wider issues of opportunism and collaboration with evil that the Nazi regime in particular but also the Stalinist regimes of the Eastern Block posed for their citizens. Questions which in neither situation can be said to have been happily resolved.

Colonel Redl explores the dilemma of a loyal, probably homosexual army officer of the Austro-Hungarian Empire whose identity and inclinations catch up with him as his dissembling about his nature is disastrously exposed. *Mephisto*, based on a story by Klaus Mann, is Szabó's investigation of a real-life figure actor Gustaf Gründgens, a left-wing Weimar actor who put himself at the service of the Nazis out of an opportunism widely adopted in Hitler's Germany. The new *Taking Sides* is the story of Wilhelm Furtwängler, conductor of the Berlin Philharmonic and examines the arguments *pro* and *contra* 'Hitler's band leader'.

Sonnenschein brings the story closer to home. Here Szabó, drawing on tales from family and friends, examines the fate of a Jewish family in Hungary through three generations. The film starts by showing the family still in the countryside, keeping an inn. Then we see them in Budapest where the next generation is growing up in the 1930s. Young Adam Sonnenschein dissimulates his Jewishness by changing his name and converting to Catholicism, so as to enter the ranks of the aristocratic élite. After the Holocaust, his surviving son enrolls as a Stalinist official and has his own harsh ethical dilemmas to deal with.

Szabó has a genius for recreating the moral and personal dilemmas of twentieth-century Central Europe. In these great films his characters have to find different ways of adapting to the impossible, perhaps not such a suprising theme for a man who himself came to maturity in Stalinist Hungary.

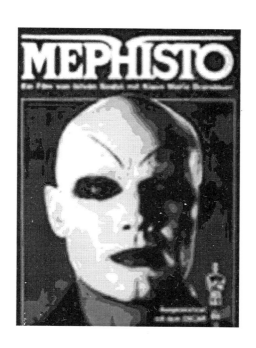

MORE

Many of Szabó's **films** are now available as DVDs:

Gustaf Gründgens, see:

motlc.wiesenthal.com/pages/t027/t02785.html

Excellent **interviews** with Szabó:

www.interfaithfamily.com/article/issue39/interview_with_szabo.phtml

www.allocine.fr/article/fichearticle_gen_carticle=708931.html

New film, *Taking Sides*:

www.guerilla-films.com/takingsides/

Count István Széchenyi

Vienna, Austria 1791–1860 Döbling, near Vienna

Genius of Reform

'The greatest Magyar' — Kossuth on Széchenyi

A nobleman but still-feudal* nineteenth-century Hungary's greatest reformer, Széchenyi burst on the political scene in 1825 by addressing the national parliament in Hungarian — a shocking innovation as the official language was still Latin. A dashing young officer, he had travelled widely and was very influenced by Britain, at that time a country in the economic and scientific vanguard. In 1830 he attacked the nobility's political supremacy — the mass of Hungarians had no political rights — and called for a reform of the old property laws. In the years preceding the 1848 Hungarian revolution against the Austrians his projects included a casino, new steamships, the Scottish-engineered Chain Bridge between the twin cities Buda and Pest, a stockbreeding association, a national theatre, a conservatory, polytechnic school and a modern ironworks. He revolutionized the nation politically, economically, technologically, fiscally and culturally — an extraordinary battery of achievements for one man. Although he opposed the national hero, Kossuth, as being a revolutionary who would upset the apple-cart of the Austrian empire, they agreed on giving precedence to Hungarian over German or Latin in the Kingdom of Hungary. However most Slovaks and Croats in Hungary didn't want to see Latin replaced as the language of administration. When a language is considered the ethnic property of one group yet everyone is obliged to use it outsiders can feel humiliated at a profound level of identity. Unfortunately the Hungarian nationalists, with their understandable fear of German, the Austrian Empire's language of education, science and central power, weren't sympathetic to the Slav position. The happy neutrality of Latin was ignored, though one of its successors in this role, Esperanto, was to have many supporters in Hungary eventually, including George Soros's father, Tivadar.

Finally, essentially over cultural issues, the Hungarian revolution of 1848 foundered. The Austrians managed to martial Croats and Slovaks against the Hungarians and Széchenyi, who had foreseen the difficulties, himself foundered. He broke down at a cabinet meeting of the revolutionary government of which he was a minister, retired to a mental hospital and later committed suicide.

In this exceptional soul the irresolvable conflicts of the century after 1848 seemed to have been played out, destroying him as they destroyed the old multiethnic Central Europe that Hungary was a part of. Today Hungary's recognised minorities, who are equipped with exemplary political and cultural rights, represent less than 2% of the population.

*serfdom persisted in Hungary until 1848

MORE

Széchenyi and **1848**

A Hungarian Count in the Revolution of 1848 György Spira (1974)

Good on Széchenyi and Hungarian history

The Hungarians: 1000 Years of Victory in Defeat Paul Lendvai (2003)

Introduction to Széchenyi:

hungaria.org/hal/hungary/index.php?halid=14&menuid=238

Albert Szent-Györgyi

Budapest, Hungary 1893–1986 Woods Hole, Massachusetts, USA

Nobel-winning benefactor of humanity (and Florida), but bad for pigs

'The key to happiness is not to get more, but to enjoy what we have and to fill the empty frame of our lives instead of enlarging it,' — Albert Szent-Györgyi

Working in Hungary in the 1930s (and he's that rare beast a Hungarian Nobel who was actually a resident citizen), Szent-Györgyi discovered or rather 'isolated', vitamin C. And hence revealed the fact that oranges are terrifically good for you. Before this they were mainly used to wash greasy plates in squalid Mediterranean inns or fed to pigs, so this particular scientific advance was tragic for porcines.

Of course it wasn't the orange that supplied the raw material in Szent-Györgyi's Hungarian lab but paprika, a vitamin-rich substance so important that it now has its own website.

Albert Szent-Györgyi was more than a self-serving absentminded professor. During World War Two he joined the resistance and supplied scientific and political intelligence to the Allies. Hitler ordered his assassination but he survived with the help of the Swedish Embassy and emigrated to the USA in 1947. He continued to do important work, some of it still controversial, on human metabolism and cancer, including pioneering studies on the role of free radicals and antioxidants, nowadays a widely studied field.

As a scientist Szent-Györgyi showed great daring, working on the principle that to be criticized by others often indicated that you were on the right track. This often led to his finding it difficult to get funding for his research. He also stuck his neck out politically, criticizing both US military intervention in the Dominican Republic and Vietnam and the misuse of scientific knowledge. In 1970 he pointed out: 'We find out how nerves work and they make nerve gas; we find out how things grow and they make herbicides.'

Szent-Györgyi is a fine example of a man prepared to stand up for his own ideas and thoughts, in both the professional and public spheres. As with so many other examples in this book, Hungary's loss of him as an emigrant was the wider world's gain.

MORE

Paprika's own website:
www-ang.kfunigraz.ac.at/~katzer/engl/generic_frame.html?Caps_ann.html
Szent-Györgyi on the **Nobel Prize** site:
www.nobel.se/medicine/laureates/1937
Book:
Search and Discovery: A Tribute to Albert Szent Györgyi Benjamin Kaminer
(1977)

Leó Szilárd

Budapest, Hungary 1898–1964 La Jolla, California, USA

Saintly inventor of the Atomic Bomb

'If I had only known that my theories would lead to the development of the atom bomb, I would have been a locksmith.' — Albert Einstein

Leó Szilárd, one of the most brilliant scientists of the twentieth century and acclaimed as such by Einstein, Planck and Heisenberg, had an infallible technique for working on problems of theoretical physics: he would lie in his bath all day, cogitating.

Chased from Berlin, then a world centre of physics, by one of Hitler's first decrees, Szilárd was rescued with around 2600 other academics working in Germany by the London-based Academic Assistance Council. Already in London Szilárd realized the possibility of atomic fission and hence the capacity to make hitherto unimaginably powerful bombs. He was in favour of keeping this a secret, suggesting a moratorium on scientific publication. But he was aware that the knowledge to produce an A-bomb still existed in Germany, then controlled by a psychopathic dictator. Along with fellow-refugee physicists Edward Teller and Eugene Wigner he persuaded Albert Einstein to get the Americans to act before Hitler did. As a result President Truman started a small atomic project in 1939. This went into overdrive after Pearl Harbour brought the USA into the war. Eventually the first chain reaction was achieved in Chicago in 1942 with the help of exile scientists from Hungary*, Germany and Italy. Szilárd said: 'This will go down as a black day in the history of mankind'. Szilárd, like most of the other physicists, was opposed to employing the bomb on a target, except as a demonstration. However the military head of the Manhattan Project that built the working bomb prevented him from speaking to Truman.

After the atomic bomb had been used on two separate cities, Szilárd dedicated himself to lobbying for a reduction of the danger of nuclear war, setting up the famous Pugwash Conference of scientists for peace and détente.

The moral of this tale is that desperate political conditions, the unrestrained rule of tyrants, cause scientists and others to act in what would otherwise be inconceivably immoral ways. Has this lesson been learned today?

* Hungarian was the *de facto* second language on the bomb projects and the US secret service had to employ telephone-tappers who spoke it

MORE

Szilárd's **book** on the abuse of science:

The Voice of the Dolphins and Other Stories (1961).

Background:

Hitler's Gift : The True Story of the Scientists Expelled by the Nazi Regime JS Medawar (2001)

Leó Szilárd Online:

www.dannen.com/szilard.html

George Szirtes

Budapest, Hungary 1948–

Poet and translator

'Szirtes is one of the best poets we have' — William Scammel *Independent on Sunday*

Widely recognized as one of Britain's leading poets, winner of the Faber Memorial Prize in 1980, the Gold Star of the Hungarian Republic in 1991 and the European Poetry Translation Prize in 1995, George Szirtes is the archetypal man with a 'foot in both camps'. Emigrating to England with his family at the age of eight in 1956, he has sought to live a parallel literary life in the pre-war world of his parents revisited as an adult and in the 'micro-Hungary' of the family home. This has given birth to a corpus of Hungarocentric poetry collected in his *The Budapest File*. Alongside this is his work that draws more on English life and explores some of the stiffness, insecurity and unease with the sensual and the passionate that one might expect.

A more expansive Szirtes though seems to emerge with the second string to his bow, his work as a translator. He has translated various major Hungarian authors, perhaps of special note the poignant novel *Anna Édes* by Dezső Kosztolányi. Somehow in inhabiting the pen of this great Magyar writer, Szirtes manages to cast aside all those emotional double-binds of Hungariness and Englishness.

In our time the age of extreme nationalism and over-emphasised national identity is hopefully mostly over. Today a boy transferred from Central Europe to England might not struggle so much with national distinctiveness, and be able to grasp with less torment the commonalties of culture that Europe and the world it so influenced share, as well as wading, as Szirtes does, in the deeper rivers of language, lyric, spirituality and curiosity all human beings traverse

MORE

Szirtes **web pages**:

www.writersartists.net/gszirtes.htm

www.bloodaxebooks.com/personpage.asp?author=George%2BSzirtes.

George Szirtes **translations**;

Anna Édes Dezső Kosztolányi (1991)

The Melancholy of Resistance László Krasznahorkai (1998)

The Adventures of Sindbad Gyula Krúdy (1998)

The Tragedy of Man Imre Madách (1988)

The Blood of the Walsungs selected poems Ottó Orbán (1993)

New Life. Selected Poems Zsuzsa Rakovszky (1994)

The Colonnade of Teeth: Twentieth Century Hungarian Poetry (co-editor and translator) (1996)

The Lost Rider: Hungarian Poetry 16-20th Century, an anthology (editor and chief translator) (1998)

The Night of Akhenaton: Selected Poems Ágnes Names Nagy (2003)

George Szirtes **Poetry:**

The Slant Door (1979), *November and May* (1981) *Short Wave* (1984),

The Photographer in Winter (1986), *Metro* (1988), *Bridge passages* (1991)

Birdsuit (1992), *Blind field* (1994), *Selected Poems* (1996)

Portrait of my Father in an English Landscape (1998)

The Budapest file (2000), *An English apocalypse* (2001)

Edward Teller

Budapest, Hungary 1908–2003 Stanford, California, USA

Bombmaker

Kiengedte, Kiszabadította a palackból a szellemet (He let the genie out of the bottle)

No, not that kind of (IRA or Hamas-style) bomb! But one of the three eminent Hungarians (Wigner and Szilárd were the other two) who contributed mightily to the invention of man's most triumphant weapon, the one with which he could destroy himself and the rest of creation (although in some accounts there would still be cockroaches).*

The story begins, if not with Cain and Abel, then when Eugene Wigner and Leo Szilard invented the A-bomb, a device of a murderous power hitherto unknown. The participation of thinking scientists, including Albert Einstein, in this invention was driven by the fear that Hitler would get there first, creating a scenario even worse than his actual achievement of the near-total destruction of Jewish Europe and the ruination of much of Christian the same — the eventual enslavement of everybody not in the pure 'Nordic' league. Later another Hungarian physicist, Teller himself, not to be outdone by his co-nationals, invented the H-bomb. Maybe this really was a 'bridge too far', but by then, yes another dictator-with-a-moustache** was scaring the living daylights out of decent folk everywhere.

To develop the H-bomb Teller — the model for Dr Strangelove in Kubrick's film about a nuclear war — had to fight with Robert Oppenheimer who ran Los Alamos where the A-bomb had been developed. Oppenheimer opposed the precipitate development of the H-bomb, seeing it as destructive beyond any military necessity. But fear of the Soviet Union proved him 'wrong'. On the other hand Teller and other scientists had demanded that Oppenheimer should get the US government to warn the Japanese about the power of the bomb before it was used on their people. Oppenheimer refused, saying: 'science should not get involved in politics'.

Teller stuck to his guns in the weapons science field, working on the neutron bomb and 'Star Wars' after the wonderful success with the H-bomb.

*On cockroaches see www.h-net.msu.edu/~nilas/bibs/appROACHES.html

**not Saddam Hussein in this case, but the 'Gorgeous Georgian' or 'Man of Steel', well known to Hungarians 1948 to 1953. What is it about moustaches and dictators?

MORE

Edward Teller **speaks:**

Memoirs: A Twentieth century journey in science and politics (2002)

How I learned to stop worrying and love the bomb:

Dr Strangelove by Stanley **Kubrick** with Peter Sellers, available on DVD

Obituary:

www.guardian.co.uk/international/story/0,3604,1039641,00.html

Build your own?

www.guardian.co.uk/g2/story/0,3604,983646,00.html

Tokay
Tokaj-Hegyalja, Hungary c1560–

A honey of a wine
Jó bornak nem kell cégér (Good wine needs no signboard)

This is one beautiful, temperamental honey of a *Hungarienne* who has turned (or spun) more heads than even the legendary ladies of Budapest. This ancient wine, interesting and unusual because of its regional and technical peculiarities, could stand for the essence of Europe, with its long traditions that are still alive and are still valued, despite all the tides of innovation our continent has seen. Tokay is special because its sweet power hypnotized Europe in its glory years, in the same way as the elegant, slightly enigmatic but often sparkfilled Hungarian personality has a way of hypnotizing the rest of us. Tokay is also one of the original 'tonic' drinks — interestingly enough, that is how the world-conquering Coca-Cola® was originally marketed.

Tokay's tonic claims are based on the fact that it's grown on mineral-rich volcanic soils and has blended into it the very sweet late-picked grapes that have undergone the 'noble rot' or *Botrytis cinerea*. Supposedly the threat of Turkish invasion in the seventeenth century delayed the harvest and the 'decayed' grapes were pressed anyway, with astounding results.

But Tokay is only the most visible tip of the iceberg of Hungarian wine varieties. Fortunately there is a strange, raving and seductive book about them by the mystic philosopher Béla Hamvas (*The Philosophy of Wine*). He uncurtains a whole curiosity box of vintages with unpronounceable names and origins and gives them delightfully 'precise' descriptions: 'An Almádi favours light lunches and afternoon snoozes. Füred wines are romantic. Arács is charming and simple. Wines from Dörgicse are the most impish of all. Those from Révfülöp find a place amongst the most authentic arbour wines…for a late afternoon in September, when one's devout friend comes over and one sits outside with him in the arbour, drinking from tiny glasses, but thick and fast. It is the wine I would recommend for letter-writing. For a love letter, of course, it would differ according to the nature of the relationship: for a passionate love only a Szekszárd will do…'*.

Oh yes, do pass the Coke®!

*This passage was specially translated by Tim Wilkinson who I thank for bringing the book to my attention. *Philosophy of Wine* is available in English in a new translation from Editio M 2000 (www.editiom.hu)

MORE

Tokay lives!

www.wines.com/tokaj/home.html

www.stratsplace.com/rogov/tokay.html

A **Tokay-lover**'s site:

www.funkcity.demon.co.uk/tokaj2.htm#5

Ignatius Trebitsch-Lincoln

Paks, Hungary 1879–1943 Shanghai, China

Adventurer, Member of Parliament and Man of God

Segíts magadon, az Isten is megsegít (God helps those who help themselves)

We are used to hearing nowadays from a certain kind of American celebrity that 'you can be whatever you want to be'. The man who lived out this dream to the fullest was neither an American (despite his first name, adopted in honour of one of the most honourable of US presidents) nor our contemporary but Ignatius Lincoln Treibitsch. He was born in a little fishing village on the Danube and moved from a rather significant spell as a drama student to writing Wild West adventures for the Budapest newspapers. Suddenly he leaves Hungary, converts to Anglicanism (in Hamburg!) and goes off to study theology in Canada, where he becomes a deacon.

He then came to Britain which he conquered via speaking tours for the anti-booze Temperance Society and, having taken British citizenship, got himself elected as MP for the Darlington constituency. His glorious career then moved on into high finance, via bankruptcy to outright forgery. His continental associations brought him under suspicion of being a German spy in the inflamed atmosphere of World War One and he was forced to flee. He achieved notoriety as a spy, an international agent, selling his services and secrets to various conflicting forces in Central Europe, including right-wing German *putschists* and the Hungarian and Czechoslovak governments. Things got too hot for him in Europe and he moved to Shanghai, that wonderful pre-war refuge whose international status meant that anyone was accepted as a resident without papers. There he enters the service of both war lords and the official Chinese government, but then, following another conversion experience, becomes a Buddhist monk. In this format he attempts to establish a 'mission of enlightenment to the West'. All this in between stealing gold watches and conning various millionaires and rich widows he meets on cruise ships.

His curious career demonstrates that 'God is all things to all men' and that, yes, you can be what you want to be. Just be prepared to lie, change your name frequently and serve any master who will pay you.

Shanghai 1930s

MORE

Shanghai the International Settlement:
theory.lcs.mit.edu/~jherzog/Masks/FFChina.htm
Secret War in Shanghai:
An Untold Story of Espionage, Intrigue, and Treason in World War II
Bernard Wasserstein (1999)
Major experimental **biography:**
The Secret Lives of Trebitsch Lincoln Bernard Wasserstein (1988)
Web **speculations and fantasies** on Trebitsch Lincoln:
www.vialarp.org/1936/doc_aimsley_letter_8.html

Viktor Vasarely

Pécs, Hungary 1906–1997 Annet-sur-Marne, France

Op Artist, beachcomber and aspirin pusher

Rend a lelke mindennek (Order is at the heart of everything)

Vasarely was the man who invented Op Art and thus inspired a thousand headachey 1970s wallpaper designs. But beyond the somewhat over-exposed glarey orange-and-browns or fluorescent turquoise eye-poppers lies a fascinating attempt to make abstract art something more than a status symbol for millionaires. As a young artist in the late 1920s, studying at the so-called 'Hungarian Bauhaus' in Budapest, he absorbed Constructivist notions of dissolving the distinctions between the materials and motives of everyday life and objects and the practice of art. Emerging from the philosophy of the early Soviet avant-gardists like Tatlin and Malevitch in the first optimistic period after the October Revolution was a strongly democratic conception of art — 'The end of a personal art for a sophisticated elite is near, we are heading straight towards a global civilisation, governed by the Sciences and the Techniques.'* For Vasarely, the rightist political climate of Budapest became uncongenial and he moved to Paris, where he eventually found a semi-official role as a modern artist both accessible and acceptable to the *République*.

Vasarely is an excellent model of a modern artist not absorbed, like many of the current generation, by a generalized but in the end merely gestural disdain for the contemporary world. He sought ways to create a visual language with the capacity to reach everyone, even inventing an alphabet of 'visual units' that could be endlessly reconfigured. Although some of his later works seem to prefigure the world of the printed circuit, his 'visual alphabet' (and a whole body of his other work) is based on non-geometric forms, inspired by a stay in Brittany where he became fascinated by the shape, similarities but ever-present individuality of the pebbles he found on the seashore.

It may be the sense of the natural behind his 'geometries' that makes his work so appealing. It was his hope, writing in 1953, that 'the new technologies will enable us to diffuse art instantaneously to the masses'. Fifty years later the internet with its strong visual capacities makes this idea much more realizable. If ever Hungary gave birth to a visionary artist. here he is.

*from Vasarely's *Notes Brutes 1946-1960* (1973)

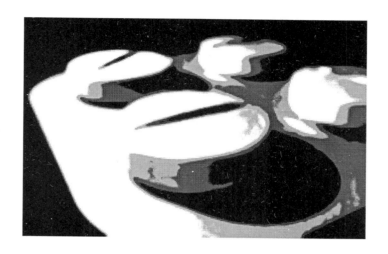

MORE

His **visual alphabet:**

www.nicola-rother.de/Vasarely.html

The beautiful **official website**:

Vasarely.org

More sites:

www.artcyclopedia.com/artists/vasarely_victor.html

www.fondationvasarely.com/biographie.htm

Museums:

Fondation Vasarely Aix-en-Provence, France:

Vasarely Museum, **Budapest**, III. Szentlélek tér 6

Stephen Vizinczey

Káloz, Hungary 1933–

In praise of older women

Az arany a sárban is arany (Gold is gold even in the mud)

In 1965 former Hungarian Revolution refugee Vizinczey wrote in praise of older women. And why not? Especially as it's the title of one of the most phenomenal bestsellers in the history of publishing, currently enjoying a second wind in French. Probably much of the success was due to its sexual frankness. It follows a young man from adolescence to early maturity in search of erotic release and tells how he hits upon the fact that older women can take an interest in a younger chap, even when those his own age tease or ignore him.

What makes this book worth looking at today is that in an age of teenage pregnancies, disrupted families and extensive emotional dissatisfaction, things haven't moved on much. Sex as a source of renewal, happiness and relaxation is still surrounded by taboo and titillation. Vizinczey's experience taught him one could learn more about sexuality — which is only 'natural' at the most mechanical level — from an experienced partner rather than another ignorant fumbler. Yet this is far from being acknowledged as common sense. A puritanical romanticism largely governs heterosexuality, based on unrealistic imagery derived from religion. As Vizinczey puts it, 'As love is an emotional glimpse of eternity, one can't help half-believing that genuine love will last forever' (p131). This 'truth' is set in the cement of consumerist materialism, which favours the social relationship of shopkeeper and client, the excitement of the initial purchase: false easiness and infantile naïveté, in the bedroom, the cinema or the supermarket.

The other ingredient in Vizinczey's eroticized *Bildungsroman* is the background of Hungary in those tough years 1944 to 1956. His protagonist first learns something about women in the strange circumstances of a refugee camp where even women of high rank are reduced to selling themselves for salami or milk powder from the kitchens of the U.S. Army. He matures in the coldest of Cold War years and provides fascinating flashes of illumination about the atmosphere of then: 'The pool in the Lukács Bath…the domain of the off-beat:.. This varied collection of people had one characteristic in common, a defiantly exuberant attitude towards life. In the worst year of Stalinist terror and fanatical puritanism, the women there wore the latest Italian-style bikinis. This would have required some daring even in most parts of the West at the time; in the Budapest of 1950, it was an act of civil disobedience. Going to the Lukács…was like leaving the country'. (p66)

After the success of his first book he wrote the social and political commentary *The Rules of Chaos* and a collection of pieces on literature as well as translating important works of Hungarian fiction. But as he says at the end of *In Praise* 'The adventures of a middle-aged man are another story'.

MORE

Translations include:

Be Faithful Unto Death Zsigmond Moricz (1996)

Elegant **web page** on Stephen Vizinczey:

www.literarymoose.info/literature/vizinczey.html

Other titles by Vizinczey include:

An Innocent Millionaire (1983)

Truth and lies in literature. essays and reviews (1986)

Also **check**:

books.reviewindex.co.uk/reviews_uk/?q=stephen+vizinczey

Now in **French:**

Éloge des femmes mures - les souvenirs amoureux d'Andras Wajda

The web addresses included in this book can be found at the Eminent Hungarians page on the publishers' website babelguides.com